DIVINE SELF

Divine Self

Awakening to Sacred Remembrance

Alania Starhawk

This book is a documentary of the author's personal experience. The information provided is designed to be an inspiration to the reader, without assuming any responsibility for the choices each reader makes in their life. Each reader is encouraged to follow their own personal guidance regarding all life choices and actions.

www.AlaniaStarhawk.com

This book is lovingly dedicated to every
sacred being who saw the Light in me
before I could see it in myself.

Contents

Acknowledgments

With great appreciation and love, I thank my beautiful mother, Barbara, for never letting me give up on my dreams. From an early age, she awakened a passionate faith within my soul. That faith is what allowed me to confidently trust in the first messages from God and the Divine. She is my angel, in this life and all lives.

It is my amazing son, Matthew, who opened my awareness to see beyond all that I imagined to be possible. As a young boy, he told stories about the worlds he could see through divine sight alone. He taught me to trust in my own visions and divine abilities—even when he had no idea that he was doing so. I cherish the privilege and gift of being his mother. *I love you, Matthew.*

My "family" also extends to all who are part of my soul tribe. So many beautiful beings have inspired me to do what I love and love what I do. They have freely listened to my many anecdotal stories in countless sessions, circles, and postings. And their feedback has allowed me to recognize the power in each one of my meaningful, and sometimes amusing, stories. I am so grateful for that inspiration, as those profound tales— and so many more—are now woven throughout these pages.

Each sacred "client" has touched me in profound ways. They have trusted me to journey through fantastic realms of discovery with them, all of which granted me sight of truly intimate and wondrous dimensions of truth. After thousands of channeling sessions, I remain in absolute awe of all that we are collectively processing, clearing, awakening, and remembering on this earth journey. We are all moving through the same stages of growth and expansion, in unique ways. I bow to each of these souls who have brought valuable insight and awareness to my spiritual teachings. They have inspired so much of what I now share.

Some of these amazing beings have become a fundamental part of my practice, my teachings, my heart, and my life. They have become friends, family, muses, teachers, benefactors, cheerleaders, and pillars of shining light. Each has directly contributed to this book's creation in some sacred way.

Infinite waves of gratitude flow particularly to MaryAnn, Andrea, Susan, Sharon, Michael, Pharon, Shannon, Erin, Kya, Natalie, Tina, Jill, and Priscilla. They have been constant forces of inspiration, love, and support throughout my book writing journey. I am so grateful for their presence in my world.

Special appreciation especially flows to the two bright sisters who have given wings to the truth of my soul. To Shirley and Margaret, I am forever grateful! I am so thankful for their generosity of heart—and creative writing skills. They have gracefully shaped the words upon these pages. And they have both inspired this book to be so much more "alive" than it once was. I am truly thankful.

With tears of joy, I also wish to thank every bright guide, guardian, teacher, and elder that has walked me through the veils of time between time. Their boundless love and faithful presence have opened realms of ineffable wonder within my soul. I am all that I am because they have reminded me that I am so. With them, I am home.

Introduction

I have danced with the universe and journeyed deep into ancient realms of sacred knowledge and truth—but that is not where I began.

I spent the majority of my life in a foggy stupor. Or perhaps *slumber* would be a more accurate term, since this is a book about Awakening.

As often happens when we are dreaming, though, I did not realize I was asleep until the precise moment I woke up. I thought I had been living this life bravely, finding the greatest measures of joy that were possible. But the truth was, I was barely surviving in a world that felt intensely constrictive.

Every day I seemed to lose more of the fire that once burned passionately within. I was moving through the motions of existence without recognizing that life could be so much more fulfilling than it was. I had learned to live small—and it was exhausting.

One fateful morning opened my eyes—*my divine sight*—in such a way that I could never close them again. I was sitting on the edge of my bed, already showered, but resisting the act of officially starting my day. My body had been filled with so much anxiety that I could have easily spent the next eight or more hours on the edge of that bed without moving.

My heart had just been broken (a story I'll share much later in this book), and my nerves had been stretched to a dangerous point of hypersensitivity. Stillness was the only thing that brought me comfort. But I needed to move. I needed to live!

It was at that precise moment, of near hopelessness, that I felt the physical embrace of an Angel around me. I felt the strength of immense wings and the softness of ethereal feathers. In this embrace, I was whole again. The sorrow, which had been completely debilitating just a few moments before, was now imperceptible. I could only sense love flowing through, in infinite measure.

If any words of wisdom were imparted to me in that extraordinary moment, I don't recall them now. I remember only one distinctly powerful awareness that rose from deep within.

I suddenly understood that this sensation of all-encompassing love was the ultimate truth. It was a reflection of our greatest immutable essence and nature. It was a reminder of who we are and what we are here for.

I remember translating that phenomenal experience into this simple and confident knowing, *"Only love is real!"*

As an extension of that focused truth, the subtle, yet equally powerful understanding was that "all else is merely a human construct and a perceived illusion."

This changed my whole perception of reality.

If something—*anything*—attempted to make me feel stressed and anxious, I reminded myself that it wasn't real. It was a construct of my imagination. A story I was telling myself.

I finally understood that my life had been shaped by beliefs that had been birthed in fear, doubt, and confusion. They were misconceptions. And as such, they could be strategically transformed with confident redirection.

Perhaps this was the first moment I realized all life was a *choice*. I could choose to resonate with all that is inspiring and uplifting, or with all that feels overwhelming and restrictive.

Remember, I was sitting on the edge of that bed because fear and anxiety had been monopolizing my thoughts. Up until that moment of divine intervention, I didn't know I had a choice. But even as I came to realize that "choice" was essentially mine, I still needed to make the millions of individual choices that would lead me into my own sacred empowerment.

That journey hasn't always been easy. I often felt as though I were standing upon the precipice between two worlds of opposing forces. One would lead me deeper into darkness and despair. The other would grant me freedom. Until I had progressed down the path a bit more, I couldn't clearly see that each of these worlds were *simply a reflection* of my own inner truths.

They were both part of me. They only felt as though they were opposing forces because I had yet to understand the nature of either. I knew I wouldn't feel safe in this world of extraordinary possibility—that which we call Life—until I had learned to understand the beauty, power, and purpose in all unique aspects of existence.

In my innocence, I began to call out for greater understanding. I sensed that there was more than I could see. And I was finally ready to push beyond every limited perception of reality to discover what this might mean. In the depths of every mounting insecurity, discouraging challenge, and overwhelming emotion, I prayed for clarity, truth, and healing to be revealed.

I opened the door for "more" to be found.

It was precisely this *primal call* to all universal source that welcomed in every miraculous experience and enlightened truth. My world began to fundamentally shift, restructuring everything that I had once perceived as inflexible and formidable.

This is the story I share with you now.

It's a story of illuminating self-discovery and awareness—and it speaks of so much more than that which is my own personal journey. It carries us all through the gates of sacred remembrance, lifting all veils and clearing all resistance.

Step by step, we move deeper into our own perfect beingness and divine nature.

Will you join me?

For more than 15 years, I documented many of my extraordinary visions, dream journeys, and conversations with Source. I wrote everything down because the act of writing helped me to deepen my relationship to Self and Source. But now, those many journals serve as the seeds of inspiration for this book.

I knew that I wanted to inspire others to shed the programmed beliefs that held them back from seeing themselves through the brightest lens of truth and awareness. So I drew upon those journals to bring life to our— humanity's—epic story of Awakening.

Each chapter contains inspired messages from Divine Spirit. These channeled messages come directly from my journals, and the quotes span more than a decade of sacred and enlightened teachings.

I use the word "teachings" throughout this book to remind the reader that these heightened understandings were originally taught to me by God, Spirit, Source, and the Divine. They came directly from my intimate relationship with Spirit

Guardians and Masters of Light upon the highest planes of conscious awareness and truth—but they are not mine.

They are ours.

Although these teachings originally came through to support my own spiritual journey and growth, I soon understood that Spirit was always speaking to all of us, as the beings of Light we are. Even when I had considered a message to be uniquely mine, and relative to whatever mountain of self-discovery I was traversing in that moment, Spirit was still speaking to every soul who would be eternally blessed.

You see, our concept of Self is quite small at times. We see our Self as the "person" we've always believed ourselves to be and cannot quite fathom how boundless and infinite we authentically are. Our energies, yours and mine, are interwoven, interconnected, and supporting each other in greater ways than can be imagined.

In truth, there is no separation between the spirit and life-force that flows through you, me, and all universal consciousness. This is the core teaching of all that I share in this book.

Through phenomenal life experiences and direct conversations with God, Spirit, Source, and the Divine, this conceptual truth has become my foundational truth. It has become my *everything*.

In these pages, I share countless stories with you. Each one carries deep symbolism and can serve to activate energetic resonance within your own soul.

Be gentle upon yourself as you read. You might not be able to race through as quickly as you had hoped. In fact, some of the precious souls who read my first draft (for creative feedback and reflection) were guided to stop reading at random points in the book, so that they might integrate the deeply encoded energies before they could continue.

I'm not suggesting that this will be your experience. I'm only suggesting that you honor whatever your perfect experience might be. Listen to your body. Honor your intuitive instincts. Approach each page as if it were written particularly for you—because at some level of unseen awareness, I trust that it has been.

It's even possible that you will see it all differently than I do, or perhaps you will see these profound truths as mere pebbles in the miraculous ocean of possibilities that speak directly to you. Trust your own voice to be your guide. As we discuss at several different points throughout our journey together, only you can know what is best for you.

This encourages me to also explain a bit about my writing style, so that you might fully understand all that is shared.

We will, in remarkable ways, be opening doors of awareness and clearing all forms of resistance to our divine nature; but we will not follow any structured timeline or roadmap to arrive at our "destination"—which is to accept and acknowledge our *Divine Self* as our most inherent and natural state of being.

You might merge deep into union with your *Divine Self* in just the first few pages of reading; but learning to trust in this union and to accept it as your absolute truth might take a bit more practice. To support this evolutionary journey into wholeness, we'll layer in a subtle foundation of conscious expansion that speaks directly to our souls.

Spirit guides the direction of each chapter and teaching, while I bring depth to each teaching by sharing my own stories of miraculous awakening. Once you read through this book fully, activating every fundamental teaching within, you'll be able to refer to it as a resource of inspiration and reflection throughout the years. It's designed so that you might be able to open the pages and be inspired by a single quote or insightful message. Because, after all, these teachings can be applied to all of life's many unexpected scenarios and adventures.

It's not a "story" that has a beginning and an end. It's an epic tale of evolutionary awakening—a deepening into Self. The more you grow, the more you'll see.

I'd also like to bring clarity to my use of capitalization. In the earliest pages of writing, I had capitalized everything—literally—to emphasize the power that was held in every thought I shared. Spirit eventually giggled at that practice and asked, *"Who are you trying to prove this to?"*

How profound! They asked me to see all of these mighty concepts and facts as common truth. And in doing so, I would empower them more. In response to their inspiration, I have used capital letters very sparingly. In fact, I've only used them when my whole body and spirit has told me to. So please do not judge the use or non-use of capitalization. If a powerful word like "light" or "divine" is not capitalized, it's because I want its undeniable power to be accepted as a normal part of our existence. I believe that this practice will help us to remove the veils of separation that sometimes keep us apart from these grander vibrations of all-encompassing wonder and possibility.

If I have used a capital letter, with purpose and intention, it most often brings attention to a collective energy or consciousness that is greater than our current human understanding. It's meant to ignite a boundless sense of grandness, within and throughout.

And the last detail of importance (that I will discuss more fully throughout this book) is my interchangeable use of these illuminating terms: God, Source, Spirit, and the Divine. I've tried to streamline my thoughts to choose only one descriptive for the omniscient force of united consciousness that is, but that just feels too limiting. So, with great measures of love and the best of intentions, I allow myself to use each of these terms as I am naturally guided to. They are all one single force of pure consciousness! The word itself means nothing. It's the energy behind it that means everything.

Please indulge this idiosyncrasy of mine. It will always be.

I started my journey by believing that God was the only source of Divine (with a big "D") presence. I had believed myself to be small, far removed, and unworthy in comparison to all that God represented. But that perception was false in every conceivable way. This book shatters those confining beliefs without ever diminishing the magnificent wonder that is God.

These stories deepen our understanding, our faith, and our connection to the Divine Light in all creation. In you. In me. In nature. In laughter. In truth. In shadow. In adversity. In doubt. In sorrow. In peace. In hope. In love.

To awaken the *Divine Self* is to awaken the beauty and perfection that has always been.

Are you ready to see your Self through the eyes of Love?

Let us begin.

CHAPTER ONE

Temple of Self

"In this and all moments, you are perfect and pure. Only perception can imply that you are anything less."

~ Divine Spirit

I remember the moment I entered into this earthly incarnation. I remember the feeling of loss that came with the new experience, as if I could no longer connect to the ineffable Light that had been my everything just a few moments before that birthing.

My own precious divinity had become cloaked within the illusion of ephemeral physicality.

As the boundless spirit that I had always been, I looked out of the newborn eyes that now housed my bright essence. I searched for recognition from those who gazed upon me. But the connection that I felt between myself and those around me was now different than it had been when I was embodied in only life-force energy. It now felt as though they were unable to see me as I truly was. Regardless of how beautiful I was to each of them, they could only see *the baby* that had just entered into this world.

1

People had forgotten how to look beyond that which was merely physical. The graceful art of *soul recognition* had been lost.

Even in those first moments of earthly awareness, I knew it. I knew that we, as human beings, could only see what was apparent and superficial. The depth that comes from remaining connected to our boundless soul awareness had been lost.

As time passed onward, I learned to deny the parts of me that felt different, alone, and unseen in my physical body. I didn't actually change how I felt within myself. I just disguised how I felt so that I might blend into the world that I was now part of.

I moved through the motions of life and soon became soothed by all the kindnesses and securities that an earthly life can bring. The physical reality that had once disappointed me in its perceived emptiness, was now distracting me from the memories of being any more than the flesh and blood person I believed myself to be.

At deeper levels, I still felt misunderstood and unseen, but I had already forgotten why I felt that way.

Forgetfulness—as a purposeful state of perceived separation and limitation—was officially anchored into my awareness. I could no longer recognize the unseen realms of existence that I had once sensed and accepted so clearly.

I believe this shift in consciousness began to progressively take place when I was five or six years old. I actually have no independent memories from before that time that are not influenced by family pictures and stories.

I've journeyed into deep meditative states so that I might retrieve the memories that I had blocked throughout those years, but I sense only one constant truth throughout that time. I was deeply focused on my internal world and personal awareness. I could not identify with the world around me, so I made no significant imprints of those memories.

My mother tells me that I was extremely quiet and "shy" in my younger years. That resonates with my memories, except I see my quietness as a natural reflection of my perceived separateness. I had nothing to say to people who spoke a different language, figuratively. But, of course, if others are unable to understand the depth of all existence, they can easily interpret quietness as shyness.

Our earthly lives, and our limited perceptions of Self, have been built upon countless misperceptions like these.

In the earliest years of my life, I felt separate from those who saw our reality through these shallow mindsets. But I eventually became one of those precious souls (because we are all *precious* in our authenticity) who could only trust in that which was surface deep.

In the first few moments of incarnation, I couldn't identify with the world around me. It felt empty and cold, as if I didn't belong. But as the memory of an alternate reality faded away, I began to intimately resonate with my physical existence as my only existence. I trusted my physical sight to guide my way, and my logical mind to explain all that might be. I was fully mesmerized by all that occupies those immersed solely in a physical reality.

I was still the wise and ancient soul that was here to understand the boundless nature of all I authentically am. I just couldn't see it.

I was walking through my life without true sight.

Even in those moments that I was able to see so much more than others could see, I couldn't accept that sight as divine. I denied my divine nature so completely that I couldn't see clearly even when I was "seeing clearly."

This can only make sense to those of you who have received clear intuitive insights, and then spent a lot of time and energy denying those clear intuitive insights. We don't know why we know the things that we know—and the thought of not knowing why we don't know is too overwhelming to our logical mind. To accept the infinite as part of our personal reality would open far too many fields of inconceivable possibility.

It takes bravery to change our perceptions of reality.

Therefore, if my wise and ancient Self was going to productively shift my limited perceptions of Self upon the physical realms of awareness, she was going to have to be a bit sneaky about it. That enlightened part of me would have to orchestrate just enough phenomenal synchronicities and subliminal teachings that I would begin to question the unknown paths of potential and possibility, within and throughout.

> *"Your soul is already free—and calls out to all that it knows itself to be."*

> ~ **Divine Spirit**

To get my attention without any "logical" interference, my soul—and all infinite aspects of my wise and ancient Self— began to call out to me in my dreams.

In dream state, these divine parts of me started to introduce sensational teachings and understandings that were far beyond my current awareness, and sometimes even far beyond my capacity to comprehend. But, because our dreams allow us to move through these alternate realities as if they were actually happening, they made imprints in my awareness—imprints that eventually started to trickle back into my logical mind in my ordinary wake state.

Yes! The reality I had so diligently created for myself in this lifetime, was now beginning to shift and evolve. The stories I had been telling myself about what was true and real were now beginning to slowly unravel.

By the time I reached this point, I was well into my thirties.

At first, I was just going along for the ride in each dream that I could remember. I was simply witnessing all that was presented, as if it were an impersonal movie that I was viewing. But as I became more comfortable in the exploration of divine truth and heightened awareness, the dreams became more lucid and interactive. I was learning to have actual experiences that could only take place within the dream state.

They were still "dreams" if I looked at them from a logical point of view; but they were real to anyone who could see these alternate planes of existence as boundless realms of non-physical truth. All that I was experiencing upon those alternate planes of consciousness was staying with me!

In some inconceivable way, *it was all real.*

For instance, if I crawled into the loving embrace of a great lion in my dreams, I retained the sensation of feeling incredibly safe, loved, and supported on the physical planes, long after I awoke. I could easily recall the warmth of his embrace, the strength of his body, and the softness of his lustrous mane, as if they were all sensations I could reconnect to with only a shift of awareness. In fact, I still feel that way about the beautiful lion that has greeted me in more than one fantastical dream scenario. He is a sacred guardian for me now. He is with me as often as I'd like him to be.

While this book contains many miraculous stories of both my physical and non-physical epiphanies, I will be speaking a lot about my "dream teachings" because so much of my heightened awareness was introduced to me in my dream state. My dreams served to expand my awareness in ways that my logical mind never could.

> *"Dreams can be incredible tools of healing and teaching for a soul who is gently awakening. In dream state, all senses are heightened and resistance to out-of-norm perceptions are minimized. Your soul can genuinely explore and participate in higher dimensional experiences—without ever challenging the accepted perceptions of reality that exist in your ordinary wake state."*

> **~ Divine Spirit**

When we are ready to see the hidden workings and mysteries of Life in new ways, Spirit will often use dreams to introduce new concepts and ideas into our awareness.

These new concepts and ideas appear as mere seeds of inspiration and insight to our logical mind, but they have the potential to grow and reach into our ordinary states of consciousness—if and when it's comfortable for our logical mind to accept a new level of understanding on the physical plane.

Once we are ready to bring these subtle, subconscious insights into our conscious awareness, they become the teachings that explain a much larger concept of truth.

For example, when I learned to stand up to irreverent bullies in my dream state equipped with nothing more than a confident faith in who I was, I was able to carry that invincible sense of empowerment back into my physical awareness. I was able to see myself as the peaceful warrior because I remember what it felt like to be the peaceful warrior in my dreams.

I wasn't just standing up to one irreverent bully on those higher planes of non-physical reality. I was theoretically standing up to *all who represented that archetype*. The dream provided an experience for me which ultimately inspired a strategic way to move through similar scenarios in my wake state.

Overall, my dreams were leading me into new and expansive realms of consciousness. And although they were quite perplexing at times, they were exciting my soul. They were teaching me to believe in something so much greater than I had known.

One particularly vibrant dream served to illuminate the recesses of my mind that had grown quite comfortable in seeing myself as insignificant.

It helped to lift me out of my own self-imposed subservience, as you will see, without ever conveying a spoken word to the logical part of me. It spoke only to my heart and soul, telepathically, in a language that was purely energetic in form.

I will share this dream with you in just a moment. But first, I'd like to stretch our minds just a bit more.

What would happen in our immediate world if we began to see ourselves as whole, empowered, and divine?

Would we see direct change and impact in all that surrounds us? Would we feel differently about ourselves and begin to see our own personal energies authentically shift and evolve effortlessly?

When we change the way we look at something, the thing we look at changes! This is a philosophical truth that has been touched upon by countless sages over the eons—and it's the exact precept that shapes my entire dream.

I ask you, *"How great could our potential be if we never first perceived ourselves as incomplete?"*

Like so many others, I had lost connection to my wise and ancient soul in this lifetime because I perceived that my environment could effectually change me. I surrendered my own self-awareness to become that which I thought I had to be.

But something was changing within me. I was ready to move beyond those empty perceptions. It was time to recognize a greater truth.

Perhaps you can resonate.

This is the journey each truth seeker bravely undertakes—to discover his or her inherent beauty through the eyes of love and acceptance, rather than judgment and expectation.

A few years ago, after an irresistible and well-deserved nap, I awakened from dream state at precisely 11:11am. I opened my eyes to reunite with the physical world I knew so well, but I was not the same person who had slipped into dream state only an hour before.

I was forever changed by all that my soul had experienced within that non-physical state of authentic being. A true sense of belonging had awakened within me and it felt as though I had become the living vessel through which all divine Light could express itself.

I was no longer bound to the single reality that had directed my whole interpretation of life and truth. I was now aware of the many diverse realities that were all intimately connected and entwined with our own, bringing balance to every unique aspect of infinite and boundless understanding. Even the concept of "imperfection" could not exist upon these planes of heightened awareness because only love governs this state of pure and perfect truth.

From that expanded point of view, all life is precious and celebrated as such.

If we accept that I had fallen deep into forgetfulness in my earthly life, but was now ready to step into sacred remembrance, we can understand what this dream was seeking to awaken in me.

It was essentially calling out to the wise and ancient part of me that was *ready to be seen.*

It was inviting me to rise through my own evolutionary stages of growth—from blindly accepted anonymity to confident states of empowered divinity!

My first lucid point of awareness, within this dream, allowed me to watch an aspect of myself welcoming various monks, spiritual leaders, and holy ones into my personal and humble home. They were in need of a space to gather, so I happily stepped aside to allow them access to all that would support them that afternoon. I felt honored to be of service in this way.

I watched each bright soul as they gracefully performed their respective tasks of making tea and preparing sacred offerings. There was an aura of ineffable peace surrounding each one of them, creating a radiance that was quite mystical and intriguing. It seemed almost as if their physical forms were free of the confining bounds that we so often attach them to.

Was it possible for our earthly reality to be this extraordinary and carefree?

I was in awe of all they were presenting themselves to be. And yet, I was amazed to notice that each of these majestic souls looked into my eyes as if I was the "holy one."

They could see something in me that I had yet to discover in myself.

Slowly, my home, which I had originally perceived as average and humble, now began to physically transform into something more extraordinary. Bright colors and intricate tapestries began to appear everywhere, even though no one was physically creating changes in the environment.

These wondrous and profoundly mystical alterations were naturally birthing themselves to compliment and honor the transformation that was taking place upon unseen levels.

The walls began stretching and reaching upward, allowing the space within this "home" to become more open and expansive, while steps to support a ceremonial altar soon became clear. I even sensed that this energy was now pure enough to welcome all wise celestial masters from the cosmic planes of being to journey with us in a sacred way.

The veils between the heavenly dimensions and our own were thinning—and the two could easily merge and entwine in the Light that was now awakening.

I remained lucid throughout this dream and was quite conscious of my thoughts and observations with each shift in energy. At one point, I had wished to share this profound moment with those I love. So, I ran to the front door, which had now transformed into one of many impressively tall doors that outlined the front angular portions of the building. I first drew aside a colorful fabric, which draped itself from ceiling to floor, and then pushed open an ornately carved wooden door.

Outside the door were countless steps all leading down, and I finally understood the transformation that was taking place. This simple and humble home was now a pure and ancient temple—a sanctuary of sacred Light.

I never did leave the building. It seemed as though my thoughts were enough to call out to every soul I loved. So, I turned back within, and became entranced by the astonishing beauty, opulence, and sanctity of each corner and recess now held within that physical space.

Every soul was still in motion, as they had been just a few moments before, but I noticed an even greater brilliance emanating through each one. As my appreciation for their beauty shifted, so did their physical appearance.

I was, in some yet to be imagined way, affecting change in this space.

I felt a connection to each element that was shifting, but I could not possibly explain it to myself or any other. As I surrendered to the energy that I knew to be real, even without logical validation of its certain truth, the transformations continued.

Colors and paint began to decorate the faces of each soul who moved freely, while strands of beads appeared around their necks. Their bodies became more elongated and their spirits seemed to become boundless and unrestrained.

Previously, each holy one had represented piety—but now they each represented the extraordinary miracle of Life.

There's a great difference between these two perceptions. One is constrained by illusive context and meaning, while the other is open to limitless interpretation.

These beautiful beings, who now appeared to be even greater than a mere grouping of individual souls, were speaking to me in ways that my mind could never comprehend. Their eyes, which served as portals into true divine beingness, opened chasms of space within my Self. They drew me deeper into my own internal sanctum of sacred knowing—a place that I had considered abandoned, lost, and gone.

And there, in the infinitesimal blink of a rapturous moment, my body shook with the power of *sacred remembrance*.

Without a physical mirror to validate the transformation that was taking place, I knew that I had become the temple that I had admired so much.

Every outward symbol of joy, love, and inspiration became embodied and alive within me. I am, and have always been, a living temple of divine Light.

And so are you.

How profound!

The physical world, within and throughout, was not as structured and formidable as I had perceived it to be. It was only a mere shift in awareness that progressively changed everything I thought to be so constant and unchangeable—which justly implies that all life is as malleable as I can imagine it to be.

Each of us is directly connected to the worlds we are a part of. We contribute to their creation without ever recognizing the power that we hold.

On unseen levels, we are more than we know.

This incredible experience allowed me to become more fully aware of my own infinite nature—the one that was actually orchestrating each subtle movement and thought.

Even when I understood that direction to be coming from Spirit and that which existed outside of myself, it was still coming from an unseen aspect of my greater all-encompassing truth. I was beginning to sense the constant and immutable connection between all infinite planes of consciousness.

They were never as separate as I had perceived them to be.

They all existed within my Self.

I can still recall the details and the emotions of that phenomenal dream teaching because my soul was entwined with every deeply encoded symbol and inspiration that was shared. My intellectual mind had surrendered to the divine frequency in play.

The same *divine frequency* is now woven through each of the simple words you read in this book. You can choose to connect to the letters on a page, or you can choose to feel the energy that is encoded more deeply into each of the letters that appear.

With this experience, I was able to fully accept my immutable perfection without doubt or resistance, because every symbolic detail spoke to much more than my logical mind. I was captivated by a pure energy that drew me deeper, step by step, into my own epic tale of self-discovery.

As we move forward through this book together, I pray that each of you look for a deeper understanding than these words, stories, and teachings can convey. I encourage you to open your intuitive awareness to the insights, synchronicities, and blessings that powerfully flow.

This book serves as a powerful portal to the higher planes within yourself and throughout all universal source. If you are ready to see with new sight, truth will be yours.

For these precious moments, I am your guide into all that might be perceived as new and insightful, but you are still the director of your journey and the creator of all you know. Allow these words and all that is shared to be the inspiration that awakens your own *Divine Self*.

> *"A sacred union is taking place between the higher realms of divine consciousness and the earthly realms of physical awareness. This allows our Divine Self and our Earthly Self to merge in exquisite harmony. With each breath, we can more easily identify with the perfection that is, both internally and externally."*

> ~ **Divine Spirit**

CHAPTER TWO

Cellular Remembrance

"From the depths of our conscious spirit, all truth is known. No essence of being can be unknown by he who is in harmony with his divine nature.

Within the One lies the Whole."

~ Divine Spirit

As innocent seekers of truth and light, our souls call out to remember. We're not exactly sure of what it is that we have forgotten, but we know that there must be more than we currently see and perceive.

On the surface, we yearn to be connected to an indefinable "it" element that will surely bring us all that we ultimately wish to find. But at deeper levels, our desires are much more simple.

We all, regardless of circumstance, wish to be safe, loved, and accepted. We all wish to be whole and complete.

As we search for ways to make this happen for ourselves, we navigate through life's many pathways as best as we can. But since we don't have clear sight for all that is, at every extraordinary level that may be, we can only make assumptions about that which we believe will bring us all we seek.

We're allowing our current understandings and interpretations to guide us, without ever acknowledging that there are many more expansive understandings and interpretations to explore.

If you truly are a wisdom keeper and truth seeker, you're probably on a perpetual search for "more," even when the concept of "more" is baffling, bewildering, and a tad bit intimidating.

We are driven by an innate desire to go beyond all that we currently know. But how do we comfortably shatter the bounds of all we've known, so that we might effectively attract and welcome that which we don't yet comprehend or understand?

This is where we recognize the distinction between logical, thought-based programming and a deeper form of foundational programming. One carries the beliefs and understandings that have been adopted and maintained through a physical path and experience. The other carries an infinite expanse of knowledge, truth, and information that speaks to our subtle bodies of energy and light.

On an unseen, cellular dimension of being, we carry the blueprint for all sacred truth. Every unique and distinct aspect of divine expression that exists within the full spectrum of divine expression is held within this subatomic library of light. It's all-inclusive, and it's stored within our *cellular memory*.

As we step into new experiences and sensations on the physical plane, this library of stored information brings all pertinent insights to the surface. All dormant understanding that is now ready to be known becomes activated with simple resonance, and effortlessly rises into our awareness through our intuitive nature.

Before my mind could acknowledge that I was directly and intimately connected to the trees, animals, and natural forces of life that surrounded me, I held intuitive visions of myself telepathically communicating with each of them. These visions brought focus to the ancient memories I held within. At some alternate realm of time and space, I already knew what it felt like to be consciously connected to all elements of our natural world.

Those memories were spontaneously rising at that moment in time because I was wanting to *feel connected* to the world around me. In response to that innate desire, the intimate memories of being connected arose from a sacred source within and communicated to me through my intuitive nature.

Our intuition is the *channel of truth* that assists us in understanding the indefinable, illogical, and miraculous within the physical planes of awareness. It keeps us connected to all unseen realms of potential and encourages us to trust our own sacred voice as an authentic channel of resource and inspiration.

I could only trust those ancient memories as real, in some indescribable way, because I was willing to trust in my own sacred voice.

Essentially, I wasn't trusting the visions. I was trusting myself.

> *"We all hold a sacred source of wisdom within, but we may never recognize this about ourselves if we don't learn to bravely trust ourselves as a sacred source of truth and divine knowing."*
>
> ~ **Divine Spirit**

It's true that in the past we've been taught to doubt our intuitive instincts and deny our personal power. But shift is happening. We're evolving! All humanity is being offered opportunities to now rise beyond the accepted paradigms and doctrines that once made sense.

I see the progressive shift happening in so many ways. On a collective scale, we are giving greater credence and value to our own instinctual nature, while simultaneously reclaiming our inherent rights to be free and independent of conformity. We are praising creativity and appreciating candor. We are wanting to rise above the restrictive patterns and behaviors that once shaped our personal experiences.

In support of this conscious evolution, Spirit is purposely using sacred symbols, sounds, and images to awaken our dormant memories. They are igniting a cellular remembrance within our light-encoded selves, to powerfully remind us that we are so much greater than we've imagined ourselves to be.

When this expansion of consciousness takes place, even in the smallest of ways, a natural doorway of possibility cracks open to welcome alternate views and perspectives into our awareness. The structured world of defined order and conformity that once served, now has the potential to become just a bit more obsolete. This gracefully loosens our indoctrinated understanding of reality and allows for new interpretations to be explored.

These new insights and interpretations can easily come from within when we first learn to cultivate trust and comfort with our own instinctual knowing. In fact, all of the many symbols, sounds, and images that appear to touch us in profound ways are most likely finding resonance with the storehouse of knowledge and truth we hold within.

For example, the outward symbol of 11:11 carries an encoded message to our energetic self that says, *"It's time to wake up!"*

In some moments, the symbol of 11:11 can appear and hold no personal value. In other moments, the symbol of 11:11 can trigger our soul to remember the greater encoding. The deeper truth always exists as a fundamental programming, but it will only connect to our current awareness when we are in resonance with that encoded message. In other words, it's not the symbol itself that speaks to us in profound ways—it's the energy encoded into the symbol.

If we each trust that there is a great unseen force guiding us and inspiring us, then it's easy to believe that our own Spirit Guides, Guardian Angels, and Higher Selves are utilizing these sacred symbols, sounds, and images to universally communicate with us on energetic levels. They are not speaking to our thought-validating minds; they are speaking to the cellular memories within our being—those that energetically whisper, *"Remember who you are!"*

Somewhere within our sacred source of truth and wisdom, we have a clear remembrance of being the priestess, the medicine man, the philosopher, the healer, and the teacher. Somewhere within our timeless and formless being, we remember that we are more than physical. We are an essential aspect of the intricate and infinite All.

As the symbols of higher perception appeared in my dream, my whole body attuned to the energies that were rising. Every shift in awareness felt familiar in some way because each was resonating with the forgotten memories I held deep within.

It was my own sacred truth that was rising!

When I saw the colorful tapestries appear in all directions, I felt the energies of power and joy awaken within me. When the ceiling rose higher and the altar appeared, I felt an energetic expansion take place in inexplicable ways. Knowing that I was part of something that extraordinary seemed to empower me and uplift my spirit.

But let's think clearly. All this interpretation happened *within*.

Not one single word told me that these people were *holy* or that this space was becoming *sacred*. No facts were offered to bring me to the conclusions I drew. Instead, I trusted an inner voice within my soul to explain and interpret all that presented itself to me.

Those bright colors would not have evoked power and joy within me unless *I already held a stored memory or belief* that interpreted these colors and fabrics in this way. These people would not have appeared as "holy" to me unless *I already held a stored memory or teaching* that classified their appearance or energy as holy.

We are continuously reacting to the world around us, without ever understanding how personal and relative the world around us truly is. We can't authentically see something outwardly that we don't already believe in.

For example, we may see a rose and smile if it reminds us of a special memory—or we may gasp and draw back if we've been hurt by its thorns before.

A rose is simply a rose. But it evokes a natural response within each of us; one that gives voice to the silent truths we hold within.

All the many perceptions, beliefs, and understandings that we've ever aligned with, regarding a rose and every other element of life, are recorded in layers within our cellular memory. But only the interpretations which resonate with our current state of accepted awareness will rise to the surface when offered an opportunity to do so.

This rightly explains how personal and relative the world around us truly is; but it also leaves space for that world to expand, shift, and change as easily as our interpretations of that world can expand, shift, and change.

When we are no longer satisfied to live in mediocrity, limitation, or stagnation, then intimate memories of being empowered, inspired, and creative will begin to awaken. These timeless truths will effortlessly rise from the depths of awareness held within, to direct our journey and shape the way we see all reality.

It's all a natural process of *resonant alignment*—which gently decrees that all which we are comfortable with becomes personal.

> *"Chasms of space are opening within you now. Chasms that lead you to your own greatest truth. Let them speak to your soul! Let them awaken the memories of all you have known. For you are 'the extraordinary' made manifest in human form."*
>
> **~ Divine Spirit**

The universe is communicating with us on intimate levels, bringing all that is supportive into our awareness.

Sometimes the inspiration they bring is clear and easy to translate into logical understanding. Sometimes it's only a mere whisper of comprehensible truth. In these moments, we can only use our intuitive skills to sense the energy held within all that is conveyed.

Although each of us stores a whole library of ever-flowing knowledge and truth within our subtle energy body, some of this knowledge defies all that we currently accept as credible and true. Our original memories of being supported and blessed lie buried beneath lifetimes of alternate views. We

21

may, in all honesty, require a bit of gentle preparation to begin trusting in the fundamental truths that now reveal themselves.

As a simple example, when I first began to sense Spirit's voice as true and real in my life, they repeated one consistent message to me over and over again. Each time I felt their presence near, they gently whispered to me, *"You are safe, and you are loved."*

They repeated these words so often that I had considered them to represent no more than a kind greeting. I hadn't yet understood that when speaking with Spirit—as a sacred and divine source—every word carried layers of information and encoding.

One day, they became a bit bolder in their kind "greeting." They told me that they would happily stop repeating these words once I accept them as personal and true.

At that point in my life, I had considered security and love to be treasured concepts that potentially existed in some unknown land, far, far away. I hadn't even realized that I had become that cynical in my view of life. But, it's true. I was a borderline nonbeliever.

Spirit generously repeated this message to me, for as long as I needed, to penetrate through all the resistance that I had built up against this fundamental truth. The words "you are safe, and you are loved" carried an energetic encoding that matched a deeply stored understanding within my soul's greatest awareness. It was purposeful. It served to powerfully wake me up, regardless of how much time it took me to do so.

Our consciousness is always expanding in brave new ways, but it sometimes requires us to be especially kind and compassionate with ourselves. We must accept that there will always be some valuable insights that lie beyond our current level of comfortable comprehension.

Our souls will only guide us forward one fateful step at a time, at a pace that honors our unique journey. If we have not yet accepted, understood, and integrated what has been shared in the first step, we won't be able to authentically layer the teachings and awareness of the next step.

It's not merely a process of "remembering." More accurately, *we're laying a foundation for remembrance to take place—*and that might take more than a brief moment of time. Some greater truths require a bit of patient preparation before we justly accept them as valid in our lives.

Sometimes a single insight activates a greater awareness within our cellular memories. It comes to inspire a new way of seeing or thinking, and cannot be fully understood until other single, but related, insights are shared. For greater clarity, we can regard each single insight as a puzzle piece that might appear entirely unassuming unless connected to other perfectly aligned puzzle pieces.

For example, I experienced a very brief, but emotionally profound vision in 2006. Its message did not become clear until I was able to trust and understand a complementary message that was shared in 2012.

In 2006, this world of higher consciousness was still quite new to me. I was confident in receiving messages from the divine realms, but many of those messages were introducing concepts that were far beyond my comfortable awareness at that time. I could only process each inspired insight as fully as I was able to.

Clear understanding of individual insights often came later, as was the case with the particular vision I share with you now. At the time I received it, I had no way of fully comprehending what was being conveyed. So I accepted it as a single, awe-inspiring experience until I was able to justly grasp the deeper meaning, in perfect time.

In the first vision, all sense of physical reality fell away to suggest that I was now in a boundless realm of timeless existence. I found myself overlooking a large expanse of desert with two pyramids farther off in the distance. These pyramids had golden light radiating from them, implying that great power and wisdom was held within.

Although I sensed light in all directions, I noticed that the stars were also alive, present, and connected to all that was being shared. My awareness was then directed to the soft sands at my feet, which began to shift and part. Before me arose a giant scarab that was content to simply rest upon the surface. As it emerged from the depths, I heard a powerful voice exclaim, *"Resurrection!"*

And with this exclamation, I snapped back to my physical reality.

All that my soul needed to receive was complete.

For years I watched the news and the archaeological sites for any signs of this great "resurrection." I had considered that my vision was a prophecy of the great wisdom and knowledge that would be discovered in some ancient site or text. This was the level of understanding I was able to embrace at that time.

Although I remained open to receive, no outer validation seemed to align with the original energy I felt. So, all remembrance of the experience had almost faded away, until my spirit was once again placed upon the boundless ethers of timeless existence to receive another puzzle piece in vision state. It was now 2012, and in just the blink of an eye, all physical reality fell away and the powerful voice returned.

This time there were no images or visions to accompany the message. There was only a reverberating thought anchoring within me:

> *"And so, it is an awakening of your own precious heart that will resurrect all ancient knowing and healing upon this earth!"*

These words triggered an instant understanding within because there was no more need to interpret everything through logical gateways. By this stage, my intuition had confidently expanded to support all that was now being shared.

Spirit was showing me that *we*, as innocent seekers of truth, would be the channels to bring through ancient knowing and healing upon the earth!

After lifetimes of valuing the knowledge and insights that came from outside of ourselves—through books, teachers, and random authority figures—I was being shown that it is time to honor and value the beauty of our own sacred beingness.

The pyramids were symbolizing our unique journeys into higher consciousness. The golden light that emanated from each pyramid represented the alchemy of our spirit and the divine frequency that can be found in all things. At my feet, the sands of Time were parted, to allow for a Resurrection of that which has always been, but had remained hidden.

My soul had accepted and interpreted all that was originally downloaded in a way that was comfortable for me at that point. But I couldn't begin to accurately interpret all that was shared until my concept of truth had expanded. And, in a perfectly convoluted way, I couldn't have expanded my concept of truth until these encoded messages had been awakened in 2006, within my subtle bodies of cellular memory.

Inspirational seeds were being planted to wake me up long before I knew that I wanted to "wake up." In fact, now I can easily see that all universal consciousness is always offering my soul an ongoing opportunity to remember. And if I'm not ready to participate in any one experience at any one particular moment in time, they will happily create other opportunities to inspire me in new ways.

It's actually the story of my life. All is possible once I am ready to receive and accept.

This lesson of opportunity and choice was even seeded into the first vision. If we look at our lives poetically, we can see that a choice is continuously being offered to us. We can choose to personally identify with the barren and lifeless desert landscape which is devoid of all creative energy—or we can identify with the golden light which permeates all things.

Neither option is greater or lesser than the other. They are only descriptive points of perception, each of which allows for a unique experience.

Interestingly, however, we sometimes choose to identify with the golden light which permeates all things, and then we create resistance to that choice by rationalizing how to get there or how to prove that we are worthy of that enlightened reality. Our soul knows how to guide us forward, but each time we allow our mind to rationalize the experience, we essentially limit our experience to only that which our mind can process and interpret. Under these conditions, we will always be bound to that which is currently understandable.

This vision teaches us that no matter what appears in our immediate world, when we are ready to authentically step beyond that which we've known, truth will rise to the surface and all sacred wisdom will "resurrect" from the cellular memories we hold within.

Without any great mental focus, we will always connect to that which we may require in each moment. As easily as we say "thank you" to someone who offers us a kindness, our deepest truths and insights will arise.

All we seek to embrace already exists within our greatest sense of Self. We are simply creating space for it to rise and express itself, with grace and ease.

I'm sure that we've each been witness to our own wise counsel when a friend or a loved one has needed a bit of inspiration. We were able to bring through the exact words, thoughts, or efforts that brought comfort in that moment, without truly understanding where the enlightened inspiration came from.

In these moments, we are trusting our *Divine Self*—the part of us that confidently knows—to bring through the inspiration that is needed.

As we learn to consciously trust this precious and wise part of ourselves more fully, the need to rationalize our choices will naturally dissipate. All we need for our unique journey will always be available because we are always connected to the part of us that confidently knows.

That is the ancient awareness that was being activated with the first vision. Although I had not been able to logically understand all the symbolism, the cellular truth had been awakened within me. I was then better prepared to welcome the next evolutionary insight, and the next, and the next— until a strong foundation of spiritual enlightenment had layered itself within.

As an ultimate truth, the brilliance that we most genuinely are can never be measured by that which is seen or recognized. For our truest light is certainly beyond that which we have the ability to comprehend.

> "To 'enlighten' is to make yourself free—boundless, infinite, and more filled with light. But this coveted state of awareness is not defined by any single point of expansion or growth. It is an ongoing process of remembering the truth of all you are. You are already enlightened, and still, you continue to become more so."
>
> ~ **Divine Spirit**

CHAPTER THREE

Boundless Me

*"Are you ready to free yourself from all you
believe yourself to be, so that you may step
into all you truly are?"*

~ Divine Spirit

With this message, Spirit is asking if we are ready to shatter
the perceptions of all we are, all we need to be, and all we wish
to be, so that we may accept the greatest unfathomable
potential of all we truly are.

My beautiful son was just a toddler when I started to have
spontaneous visions of my past lives. It's natural for me to
accept that we've all had hundreds and thousands of
individual lives now, but there was a time that this concept
confounded me. How can I have more than one life if my soul
will go to heaven when my body dies?

My understanding of a limited heaven was tethering my mind
to only this conceivable moment. In order to explore my truly
boundless Self, I had to break beyond that. So, I gently started
to spontaneously recall the intimate memories of my past
lives.

Each evening, as I laid my son to sleep, I found myself
surrendering to a deep meditative state. I was only focused on
putting him to sleep, but my mind was open enough to

welcome in my own ancient memories. At first, I thought I was daydreaming. But I was the center of each amazing story line. Each vision also included undeniable sensory perception and emotional attachment. These weren't mere dreams; they were my own personal memories.

This was my first introduction to past lives.

In one of these original visions, I was walking through a small Japanese garden. I could see my small, bound feet wrapped in pink silk. I could sense that the garden was my only respite from the cruelty of that life. I knew that I didn't have the freedom to choose my own journey. My husband saw me as no more than a belonging that he had no respect for. He kept me closely guarded and isolated from the world that existed outside those garden walls.

It was all so very intimate and relatable. In each of the visions that continued to present themselves, I always knew more than I could rationally explain; even when the scenes and scenarios revealed truths that existed far beyond that which was familiar to me.

My understanding of past lives has grown exponentially since those first moments. They are now an intricate part of the healing work I do with each of my clients. But in those early days of awakening, I wasn't yet able to see the power that they held. I was still only a witness to all that they revealed at deeper levels.

To quiet the parts of my mind that were perplexed, I asked Spirit to explain how *past lives* were even possible. If we "go to heaven" when we die, as I had been taught since I was young, how could I be intimately connected to all that was now revealing itself?

In response to my curiosity, Spirit first reminded me that *heaven* isn't a physical place. It's a state of enlightened awareness that allows us to be intimately united with all that is.

At the end of every life experience, when our boundless spirit leaves our physical body, all perceptions of separation fall away and we return to our divine state of awareness. We remember the truth of all we are and all we are connected to, without exception. This is *heaven* to all who can see clearly.

This information may or may not be entirely comfortable for you now. But I am including it in this teaching because it helps to illustrate how basic my spiritual understanding was when I first started to awaken to enlightened truths in dramatic ways.

After clarifying the greater truth of heaven to me, Spirit then showed me the boundless expanse of all that can be considered "time and space" from a divine point of view.

In the midst of that infinite plane of potential being, they also pointed to the nearly imperceptible speck of time and space that would represent this particular life for me. They inspired me to recall, from a sacred place within, how ludicrous this concept of truth would be. Why would I be divinely created to live for a mere moment of time, in comparison to the fullness of all that was and could be?

My understanding of Self was flawed.

It had been created by false truths and illusions.

Without knowing what this new perception really alluded to in the grander scheme of existential beingness, I was now more open to see beyond all that I had ever known—and this is no small statement.

I was soon recalling intimate memories of myself in ancient Atlantis, Lemuria, and more. I was walking through memories that had long been forgotten to all mankind—ones that could not be placed on any modern map or calendar.

I had, in truth, progressed into a familiar relationship with my own boundless being.

No matter how much we learn and discover about ourselves, we will always continue to expand, evolve, and move forward in new and fascinating ways. We must, simply because the One—our omniscient Self in a state of Oneness—can bravely explore itself by experientially stepping into the Self; but the Self cannot truly know itself until it returns, wholly, into the One.

Let's simplify this by accepting that the One is the embodiment of everything and can never be any less than the embodiment of everything. It can be called many different things, like God and Source, but it still can only be that which is inclusive of everything, both manifest and unmanifest.

The Self, in comparison to the One, is an embodiment of only that which it believes itself to be.

Essentially, it is only a shift in consciousness that allows us to believe that we are the all-encompassing One or the individual Self, but that shift shapes our whole understanding of personal truth.

Even when the One—from a perfect state of all-encompassing truth—becomes the Self, it sustains the awareness of simultaneously being the One and the Self. Its nature is to be all things, so even the exploration of individuality is still an intricate aspect of itself. It can still know itself as the one who is searching without ever diminishing the boundless knowledge it contains upon alternate planes of awareness.

Contrarily, the perception of truly being separate from the One—as the individual Self—can only be known from a limited state of consciousness. It can only be intimately experienced from the viewpoint of the individual "I" persona.

This is where most of us hold our current awareness, as the one who can sometimes feel separate, alone, and powerless in our experience. However, this limited awareness that creates the illusion of separation from the One is not designed to disempower the Self. It's only designed to encourage *free expression* and *open exploration*, allowing the Self to actively create without the bounds and confines of all it has previously known.

Whether we see our Self as one who is infinite and exploring our fullest potential with clear sight and awareness, or as one who is searching to remember who we truly are—the power lies within.

All that exists within the One remains whole within the Self. It's only a *perception of separation* that implies something less.

This is an important insight. It suggests that even though we may believe ourselves to be a bit lost and without direction at times, we actually hold the knowledge, wisdom, and truth of all Life within. We are never without access to the inspirations we seek.

But what is it that we truly seek?

It seems to me that each question only leads me deeper into the greater depths of unfathomable mystery. And yet, in that space of unknowable truth, I find peace.

It's a paradox, I know.

This thought—trusting that it is in fact a paradox—gives me permission to be comfortable with not knowing everything. It's actually the wisest way to move through my experience, because some of the greatest truths are absolutely "unknowable." They lie upon the infinite planes of awareness, beyond the bounds of all we can currently fathom and imagine.

Our souls are ingeniously designed to carry us deeper into those unexplored realms when we are ready to do so; to discern truth for ourselves, in our own way, without the restrictions of all that once made perfect sense.

This is exactly what was happening to me when my past lives spontaneously presented themselves and ancient guardians became my intimate acquaintances, as I will explain in a moment. I was moving deeper into the infinite planes of my own self-awareness.

For many years, while my mind was learning to be at peace in every unique and unexpected situation that appeared, I repeated these very powerful words to myself: *Let your soul explore. Let your senses soar. Let your heart know true peace in what you find.*

I was giving myself permission to move through life without prejudice and fear. I was learning to appreciate the unique beauty, or at least the purposeful presence, of everything that appeared.

If I could accept that there was no place else I needed to be to avoid the uncomfortable aspects of life, then I could begin focusing upon the intuitive way through each moment of struggle.

And so it was with that innocent focus that I welcomed my own *Divine Self*—the part of me that could always see clearly—into my ordinary reality. I expanded my perceptions of truth until I became the one who no longer needed physical sight to secure my way through life's many adventures.

Remember, we can never be without the necessary resources, emotionally or physically, to guide us through each new moment of expanding self-discovery, because all knowledge, wisdom, and truth is always ours to tap into, as needed, once we are able to trust it as real.

"A soul designs their challenges, so that they may have the privilege of moving themselves beyond their own self-imposed limitations."

~ **Divine Spirit**

Beginning in 2002, all that I had placed my trust into suddenly fell away, causing me to re-evaluate every nuance of my existence. I wasn't just asking to understand the complexities of my own challenging experiences—I was desperately seeking to understand the purpose of all existential Life.

Questions were rising from a primal depth within. They were curious and philosophical in nature, giving space for all hidden mysteries to be effortlessly revealed. Never did I imagine that these were the questions that would directly unlock the gates of my own expanding consciousness.

This was the beginning of it all—before every transformative dream, past life vision, and divine channeling. I was simply a girl, feeling lost and alone.

I moved through each day as routinely as I ever did, and then spent my nights calling out to God.

On the surface, my words were only asking "Why?" in dazed cries of desperation. But on a deeper level, they were asking for clarity, understanding, and truth in forms that earthly logic could never provide.

I was asking to understand *everything* that could possibly be, like one who needed knowledge as much as she needed breath. And in my innocence, I was trusting my faith to bring me all my soul required.

From an early age, I had fallen in love with the adoration of God, as I understood "him" to be. My faith was pure, but not completely traditional by church standards. I was raised Roman Catholic, but I communicated directly to God without needing any formal prayers or intimidating doctrines to prove my love and appreciation for the Divine.

I didn't follow the ecclesiastical guidelines that were laid out for me as a "practicing Catholic," but my understanding of God was still primarily shaped by all I had been taught in the church. I couldn't yet imagine the fullness of all God truly is.

For example, speaking to God in my times of need was natural. It was all I knew. But receiving direct responses to my prayers was not. My faith was merely conceptual at that time, and I had no idea that it could be any other way.

Miraculously, though, I began to recognize clear and direct responses to every question I proposed. Something was now different. In the stillness of those dark nights, God's voice was speaking to me—*and I was listening.*

This was a completely new experience for me. And yet, I found myself trusting this new form of inspired communication as if it was entirely natural. Each unexpected message was speaking directly to my heart, igniting a passionate part of my soul that had almost buried itself in hopelessness.

It's difficult to explain how mere words that flow through your ordinary mind-space can suddenly appear to come directly from God and Source. But this was a strong, intuitive knowing that I was unwilling to doubt.

This divine connection, which was spontaneous and un-prompted, was healing my heart. It was awakening hope in the most beautiful parts of my soul. And it was soon clear that all perceptions of struggle, lack, and challenge in my life were *self-created* and *illusionary.*

From a divine state of awareness, only love is known.

I decided to begin healing my diminished self-worth by asking to see myself through God's eyes. Innocently, I held a single prayer in my focus. It felt gentle and unassuming to me, but it began to shatter all limited perceptions of truth.

My continuous prayer became:

"Remind me of who I truly am."

This is when the transformative dreams, past life visions, and divine channelings came into my experience. In response to this heart-felt prayer, a miraculous new world of divine frequency opened itself up to me. I had trusted God to support my journey and guide me forward, but my experiences were moving far beyond anything my traditional faith could explain. Something truly epic was unfolding for me.

At first, my miracles could be easily accepted because they aligned with the beliefs and principles I had always known. But, then, an expansion took place.

Without any conscious effort or intention, Buddha, Isis, Vishnu, and other great beings of Light presented themselves to me as personal guardians and teachers. They were each reminding me of the mastery that was awakening deep within myself; but more subtly, they were also challenging my concept of God and Truth.

With each new communication that flowed, I still sensed the same indescribable presence that I had always sensed when communicating with God. Each sacred teacher was the same precious embodiment of immutable love and infinite spirit that I knew God to be.

God was still present in all that now appeared! All that was progressively shifting for me was the way in which I accepted God as an all-encompassing Light.

I was being offered a rare opportunity to see this divine presence, authentically, in new ways.

Although God—as the One—had always been this infinite expansion of miraculous wonder and omniscient being, I was only beginning to stretch my personal awareness beyond all that I had known. Just as I was expanding my sense of Self into new realms of boundless being, my understanding of God was evolving too.

I was slowly learning to recognize divinity in all things, regardless of appearance.

Even though communicating with the Egyptian deities, Isis and Osiris, was far beyond my indoctrinated belief system, I trusted in the energy that flowed. I looked for love in each teacher's embrace, instead of a logical validation for what was considered "right or wrong."

What I discovered, as I listened to each of them in their own way, is that we are all much more connected than I ever knew.

"We are each an extension of the same divine Light, reflecting in different ways."

~ Brother Buddha

There were many teachers who presented themselves to me, all offering their unique inspirations and insights. But I wasn't just learning that these bright beings existed; I was learning that they have a *personal* and *valued* relationship to me.

This was an epic understanding for someone who had always humbled herself before all forms of perceived divinity.

For example, I have always felt a close affinity to Blessed Mother. Throughout my life, my heart would soften to simply think of her Light. And I could confidently say that I prayed to her almost daily over the years. I conceptually felt Blessed Mother's presence and support in my heart, but I had no validation of that intimacy in my physical life. My adoration of Blessed Mother, for the first 30 years of my life, was entirely based on faith.

It was during a moment of deep emotional release that she first introduced herself to me in a way that I could rationally—*upon an intuitive plane*—sense, feel, and understand. She stilled all the doubts and insecurities that were underlying, so that I could truly accept the immense gift of Love that she wished to share.

One afternoon, through tears of sorrow, I sensed a compassionate touch upon my right hand. As I shifted my awareness to sense what was happening, I noticed Blessed Mother kneeling beside me. She held my hand securely, with a mother's love, reminding me that I was supported and cared for.

Her compassion was pure, and effortlessly melted the pain and sorrow I had been feeling just a few moments before.

In her embrace, I surrendered to the healing and grace. But my beliefs were not yet broad enough to accept this experience as absolutely "real" in every way. I was confident in all that I was seeing and feeling. I just couldn't understand how it could authentically be.

My curiosity wished to understand more. In fact, I wanted to heal the intellectual parts of me that still considered all of this to be a sacrilege.

Who was "I" to allow Blessed Mother to kneel beside me?

And with this thought, she telepathically reminded me that we are eternally one Light within the higher planes of truth. She knelt beside me to remind me that I do not shed a single tear alone. She has always been with me, listening to every prayer and guiding every step.

She reminded me that my mission on this earth plane is to live in love, to disempower all resistance to that love, and to awaken the remembrance of being One.

> *"All shadow, separation, and limitation can only be illusion. In the heart of Love, there can only be Love."*

> **~ Blessed Mother**

Blessed Mother compassionately lifted me out of my own blinded perceptions of Self to remind me that my soul's journey is greater than I can perceive.

I am not insignificant.

I am vital to all humanity's awakening.

And so are you.

As we each step into our own *Divine Self*, we are stepping into the fullness of all we are. Slowly, all old and outdated identities will begin to lose their value, while new and uplifting aspects of our boundless nature find expression and voice.

I never dreamed of seeing myself through such extraordinary measures of love. But now I know that even this miraculous perception of myself is still only a shallow view and understanding of my truest divine nature.

There is always a greater understanding that lies beyond our current levels of comprehension.

> *"Your Light has touched all creation and continues to do so, even in this existence. You are no less now than you have ever been."*
>
> **~Divine Spirit**

CHAPTER FOUR

Infinite Potentialities

"As you unlock the doors to let more light in, you will create more space for your own light to expand. Each time you are brought to the edge of your awareness, you will go further. It's the natural order of Life and Light."

~Divine Spirit

Rarely do we, as indoctrinated beings, process any single moment with fresh eyes and fresh sensory perception. In fact, we usually relate all newly presented information to reminders of prior moments gone by, and then naturally envision our past re-creating itself before we ever recognize that this is a *new* moment.

All moments, without exception, are independent of the last, and the next.

But we, as creatures of habit, instantly see ourselves catching a cold if we are caught out in the rain without an umbrella; we see ourselves being hurt by another the moment we lower our defenses to trust them with that which we value most; and we see ourselves growing old and frail before we ever show signs of doing so.

We are each habitually creating our future, *yet-to-be-determined realities* using a set of guidelines and parameters we've adopted from past experiences that may no longer support and serve the beautiful journey we currently find ourselves upon.

Even in the gentlest of ways, we schedule and design the outline of our days before we ever awaken to that new day. We impose arbitrary bounds upon each new moment by assuming that we already know how it should or will be.

A few years ago, I awoke one morning feeling a bit anxious about the full day I had ahead of me. Spirit whispered to me in the quiet of those early morning hours, *"You know, today can be anything you choose it to be."*

Those words both perplexed me and excited me.

It was natural for me to prove why my day needed to be busy and without flexibility. But they were stretching my awareness to now remind me that I could powerfully shift my day and introduce more inspiration and joy into it, if I so wished.

This new insight allowed me to creatively explore the many possibilities. Could I gracefully free myself from some commitments that no longer felt inspiring? Or could I be a bit more playful about the obligations I did choose to honor? Perhaps I could even learn to joyfully sing my way through each mundane task that awaited.

If we imagined that this day, week, month, or year could be anything we choose it to be, what would we truly give ourselves permission to create and experience? Would we begin to live as if there were no guidelines, limitations, or boundaries?

Our inherent nature is to move forward, to express ourselves freely, and to spontaneously create anew with each passing breath. But because societal expectations and paradigms have indoctrinated many of us to follow the well-worn path, we often doubt our instinctual nature, which thereby limits our own creative abilities. We neglect to acknowledge the sacred power we hold within.

However, I do believe we are in a pivotal state of human evolution.

We clearly recognize that there is room for change in many of the outdated traditions and customs that no longer inspire us; and we're instinctually trusting ourselves to be the source of that change by simply sharing our thoughts, prayers, visions, insights, talents, and abilities without censor.

We're gradually accepting that "who we are" is enough to shift the tides and lift the veils.

> *"Once we free ourselves from the limited perceptions of an inflexible mind, all infinite potentialities become possible."*
>
> ~ **Divine Spirit**

From a state of higher consciousness, it is no longer comfortable to accept any single set of dogmatic boundaries or guidelines as an absolute truth that fits all moments.

We have the right to discern and decide which perspective of truth aligns with us in each independent moment; and if "truth" is the element that we most honor and treasure upon our journey, then we must also recognize that there are always infinite truths that simultaneously hold value.

Life is in motion and requires flexibility from all who wish to move forward with it effortlessly.

We once believed, as a society, that a woman's place was in the home, that big, juicy roasts were the makings of a strong body, and that kids should be seen and not heard. These, and countless other outrageous assumptions, were once considered to be acceptable norms. They all wove together to create our societal paradigms.

But as our comfort levels shifted as a society, and we no longer wished to settle for those experiences as the accepted norm, our collective consciousness evolved and progressively welcomed new experiences to better harmonize with our newly chosen frequencies. All outdated paradigms became systematically replaced by new and updated versions that more aptly reflected our most current state of societal consciousness.

Most wondrously, it's also important to note that all newly accepted norms are originally pioneered by brave souls like *you* and *me*.

Even though we don't always set out to make that kind of impact upon our surroundings, we do so naturally. We, as members of society, are the *gateways* for all new paradigms and potentialities to be birthed. We are that extraordinary!

We are the bringers of societal shift and change. *Always*.

It is our own creative thinking that allows us to explore new and uncharted realms of wondrous being. When we are no longer bound by every "should" that wants to entertain our logical mind, we'll marvel at that which can potentially be.

> *"There are infinite planes of existence that all co-exist in perfect harmonic resonance. Layer upon layer, each plane interconnecting only where all is in matching frequency. As you are ready to appreciate greater truth, greater truth*

arises from within the sphere of infinite potential that always is. Every perception of reality is subjective, not imposed."

~ **Divine Spirit**

Our experiences, and all that we participate in, are merely reflections of our current resonating truth. That "truth," as formidable and constant as it may appear, has the capacity to authentically shift, evolve, and expand as often as our thoughts can shift, evolve, and expand.

It's always subjective, and reflective of that which we accept as *personally relative.* In other words, my truth can be completely different than your truth.

As an example, I once believed that life was inherently complicated, challenging, and filled with impending disappointments. No matter how positively I strived to look at life, there was always another disturbing matter to defend myself against.

It wasn't always the way I saw life, but for a long moment it was all I could see.

Each time I found my way through an unexpected or cruel life scenario, I believed that it was my strength or my wisdom that had saved me. I believed that I was doing my best to triumph in a world that was inherently challenged. But in truth, I was only contributing to the challenged world that I had come to believe in.

The world had become challenging because that's what I believed.

I couldn't see through the illusion yet. I couldn't see through the false perceptions that made perfect sense to my wounded spirit. But at some level, there was a part of me that had grown fiercely tired of trudging through the obstacle course that had become my life—and that changed everything.

One day, while walking through the trees in a nearby park for quiet reflection, I innocently listed all my requests and prayers for the year before me. Feeling a bit lost and without direction, I was passionately asking all universal source to save me from the intensity of life, and all that felt so overwhelming.

In that space of vulnerable authenticity, something primal rose up from within me; I was ready to move beyond the concept of "being saved." I was ready to reclaim my own fantastic power and potential.

I stood strong and empowered amongst those trees that now appeared to be more than mere "trees". They were now supporting me and instilling me with new measures of confidence.

I spread my arms out far and wide, and I screamed to the universe, *"I will no longer prove how strong I am! I am ready for the easy and effortless path, and I will accept no less."*

These words held power. They redefined my foundation of reality and shattered every perception of resistance that may have been. From that day forward, I saw fundamental shifts in the nature of all that life could potentially be for me.

Yes! I had finally understood that Life (with a big "L") was shaping itself to match and reflect my own chosen beliefs.

From that moment on, everything became brighter. The struggles that would have normally presented themselves were nowhere to be found! The path before me was effortlessly *clearing itself* to welcome in greater measures of support, grace, and ease.

Could it really have been that easy to change my truth, and thereby change my reality?

When I look back upon the whole experience, I clearly see that the miracle of Life was always available to me. It existed—*as a perpetual opportunity*—upon a dimensional plane that could only be accessed through resonance.

In other words, *I needed to believe it before I could see it.*

Spirit tells me that connecting to a supportive and inspirational path is like tuning into radio waves. All of the many dimensional planes of awareness are perpetually available for us to tune into (just as all the many radio frequencies are simultaneously available), but we can only receive clear information from the channels and frequencies that we focus upon. If we aren't tuned into the resonating frequency, we will only hear static and white noise. *It will all be meaningless.*

As a gentle insight, however, we must also acknowledge that the energies and frequencies that make no sense to us personally, might be pivotal and life-giving to another.

When I was believing that life was inherently challenged, I had a hard time believing in the easy and effortless path.

Instead, I was *attuned* to the complexities of life and couldn't see beyond them. But the moment I claimed personal resonance to the easy and effortless path, with that powerful invocation, my reality fundamentally changed. I energetically attuned to the supportive blessings without ever understanding the immensity of all that had just shifted.

I never changed the world that existed outwardly!

I only changed how I connected to the world that existed outwardly.

This is why we can say that every path is a "blessed path."

This is not to suggest that every path is inherently filled with inspiration and comfort—*but that every path is as blessed as we allow it to be.*

There is no need to search elsewhere for that which we seek. It's entirely possible to stand exactly where we are, as I did in the middle of those trees, and open ourselves to the blessings and support that already flows upon unseen levels of awareness.

Once we are attuned to the greater blessings, the physical path might actually change to support us in greater ways, but it's never the physical path that is responsible for the blessings that appear. It's only our confident faith in the "blessed path" that transforms every path into one that inspires and uplifts.

By acknowledging that our reality is unique, personal, and self-created, we can learn to take responsibility for the thoughts and belief systems that shape our direct experiences. If any concept no longer resonates with the journey we wish to know, then we hold the power to shift our focus—and therefore our perception—of reality and truth.

To illustrate this concept clearly, let's imagine that one hundred radiant souls were gathered together for a beautiful celebration. Each soul naturally processes the details of that experience according to their own set of beliefs, interests, and memories. They attune to their own perceptions of reality and connect to only that which is personally relative to them.

Even though all one hundred souls are united in the same physical experience, no two souls will have a perfectly mirrored experience. Each soul will have their own unique view of it all.

Their fields of knowledge and subjective interpretations will always be reflective of all they've assimilated during their respective life experiences. *Each soul can only perceive the information that resonates with their personal perceptions of truth.*

They won't even notice that which is not relative to them.

As an example, I've been to restaurants where my dinner companion was highly triggered by some source of noise that might be present. Once they regarded that noise as a disturbance, they found it very difficult to focus on feeling safe and supported.

However, because it has always been natural for me to tune out disruptive noise, I was rarely affected by those exact same environmental triggers. Often, I never even noticed the excessive sounds until one of these beautiful friends pointed it out.

I am not a better person for not noticing. I'm simply not programmed to recognize that disharmony.

I would, however, feel greatly triggered if those restaurant tables were too close together and I felt trapped. That perception may be irrational to others, but it would be truth to me. My heart would start racing, and I would have to remind myself that I am safe and loved, even in that crowded place.

We each have our own perceptions of reality, but if we learn to see these variations as potential truths that we can choose to tune into, if we wish, we might begin to reinterpret all that we perceive as "real" for ourselves.

To give my courageous son the thrills that excited his soul, I used to run, literally, to the front of every roller coaster line with him. I made sure that he was buckled into that sensational ride—and then I crossed over to the other side of the track to wait for him to return. We did this over and over. It was the only way I was able to comfortably support him.

But one day, while standing on the other side of the track, I answered a phone call from a friend. I told them where I was standing and they replied, *"Why do you hold yourself back? Fly, Sister! Fly!"*

Those words spoke to me. I never imagined that I could interpret this ride as an opportunity to feel free.

Because of some outdated programming that I still held within, I only resonated with "the fall" that every roller coaster surely included. I never imagined that even "the fall" was only a perception! I had thought it was a fact that others were comfortable with, when it was actually only my personal view of it.

The idea of flying outside of my dream state became exciting. My perception shifted, and I was ready to explore roller coasters a bit more confidently than I had before. (On a personal note, I still am a cautious rider who needs to feel my way through each twisted opportunity, but I have certainly ventured to new heights, and I intend to keep that trend going.)

The point is, Life is filled with infinite potentialities—and we are only limited by the assumptions of our own tethered imaginations!

If you are ready for change, make space for boundless curiosity. Allow the miraculous to become an intricate part of your personal reality.

As we bravely set ourselves free from all fathoms of structured conformity, so our world morphs to reflect the imaginings of all we allow ourselves to be.

Life is in motion. It breathes, expands, and gracefully explores all new realms of possibility. Accept its invitation to spiral into ecstasy.

> *"You are stronger than you know, wiser than you can imagine, and more beautiful than you can fathom! You are the MIRACLE of Life—and you are only beginning to discover what this means. Trust yourself to confidently explore all paths of extraordinary blessing. For you are worthy of so much more than you can currently dream of."*

> ~ **Divine Spirit**

CHAPTER FIVE

Sacred Source

*"You are the One to bring change, to light
the world, to brave new paths, and to ignite
all creativity into sacred beingness. You
are the One to sense deep truth and inspire
joy, within and throughout.*

*You are the One to BE THE ONE as only
You can BE."*

~Divine Spirit

Imagine, for a moment, that you are the center of all creative life-force, and all existence begins and ends with you.

Now consider that your acceptance of this ultimate truth has no effect upon its fundamental nature. In other words, it's entirely possible for you to be the most empowered force of creation at one level of awareness, while simultaneously holding the belief that you are insignificant and disempowered at some other level.

We are complex beings! We are more than we imagine ourselves to be and we are only beginning to comprehend what this truly means.

Spirit teaches me that every *master creator*—one who is aware of their own creative power and ability—must accept three primary truths about themselves and the world around them before they can begin to comprehend the fullness of all they are.

In their simplicity, these truths say it all.

The *first truth* states that each wise soul must confidently acknowledge and accept that there is more than the mind and the eyes can see. There are infinite planes of physical and non-physical reality that simultaneously co-exist with their own current perceptions of discernible truth.

The *second truth* states that they must confidently acknowledge and accept that they are intimately related to all that exists upon every alternate plane of awareness. There is always a direct connection between themselves and all that is, both seen and unseen.

The *third truth* states that they must confidently acknowledge and accept that they hold the power to effectively co-create with all that exists upon those infinite planes of awareness. There is already a supportive relationship between themselves and all universal beingness.

I'm trusting that we all accept the first truth already. That is why we are currently diving deeper into these sacred mysteries together. The last two truths have inspired me to share everything that I am now sharing, in depth. They are the foundation for this entire book.

In the full spectrum of boundless creative potential, all is infinitely possible and available to us as a sacred resource of support and inspiration. Even when we are unaware of all that we are connected to, those connections exist. As a fundamental aspect of *oneness*—the understanding that all life is interconnected—we are able to access them all at will.

We are never confined to only that which we can currently see and understand. There is *always more* to discover and explore, once we are open and receptive to the concept of "more" existing.

Imagine that we have a bird's eye view of a well-illustrated building blueprint. All details seem to be clearly marked and noted appropriately upon the sketch before us. It allows us to feel as if we have a confident understanding of the building at hand.

But as we look more closely around the edges of that blueprint, we realize that this page of the blueprint is limited to only the main area of the building. Because our awareness was solely focused on the illustration before us, we did not immediately recognize that expansions to this primary blueprint already exist.

It would be ignorant to assume that we understand the entire building intimately when we've only been witness to the first page of its design.

At first, only the architect of the plans can have a full understanding of every layer that co-exists; but our own awareness of the building will continuously expand with every new detail and page that arises.

Imagine your own life in this way.

The blueprint for your entire life experience exists, in minute detail, at various levels of awareness—like the pages of a building blueprint.

As the supreme architect in our life, our *Divine Self* has full awareness of every intricate layer of detail and design that authentically is. But we, as the ones who have forgotten our divine nature, may only have a limited awareness of our own greater truth.

Our full *divine blueprint*—remembrance of who we truly are—already exists. It includes every detailed point of varying awareness for our soul's journey. It honors that which we currently understand ourselves to be, as well as that which we have yet to imagine. It miraculously tells the story of all we are, seen and unseen, and merges all infinite aspects of our individuality into one all-encompassing matrix of immutable truth.

Most importantly, it's always available to us.

Only a shift of awareness can bring illumination and remembrance to each intricate and expansive aspect that had previously remained cloaked in forgetfulness.

In fact, we are collectively shifting our consciousness so rapidly at this stage of awakening because our current journeys of self-discovery are calling the divine blueprint back into our focused awareness. In response to our curiosity about what lies beyond our current understanding, our *Divine Self* is orchestrating miraculous synchronicities for each of us to explore.

Can you sense how true this is in your own life? Can you sense an unseen force guiding you deeper into your own self-discovery?

This is a personal journey for each of us.

We are the only ones who can know what is most comfortable for ourselves in each new moment. We are also the only ones who have direct access to our own dormant memories of purpose and power. *We are the only ones who can awaken the truth we hold within!*

I, for example, am on my own journey of spiritual awakening. I have been inspired by amazing people, wise teachings, and beautiful sights. But none of these factors can claim responsibility for my personal growth because they have only "inspired change" in my life.

In other words, my reality can only be affected by the experiences I choose to interact with. No matter how miraculous an inspiration might be, it can never directly alter my reality. It's only my reaction to each inspiration that creates positive shift and change in my world.

As I explain this, I am thinking of my beautiful son. I inspire him to follow his dreams and explore his boundless potential, but only he can transform those enlightened inspirations into a manifest reality. Unless he responds to them in some purposeful way, they will have no impact upon his precious experience. At best, my passionate enthusiasm can only be a catalyst for change. It will always be his personal choice alone—to respond or not respond—that directly shapes his life.

This principle holds true even for the teachings held within this book. They represent truth and power for me, personally, but they can only serve as an inspiration for you upon your journey.

At first, as you read the words upon these pages, you are witness to my personal story. But as you naturally react to all that you read, you are creating your own personal and intimate relationship to each of these concepts.

The moment in which you *respond* and *react*—in your own unique way—is the moment that you become the one who designs your own experience. At that pivotal point, you become the *empowered architect* in your personal journey.

To further illustrate this teaching, let me tell you about a book I purchased many years ago. I carried this book home with great anticipation. But when I began to read it, I could not connect with it. The words I read were meaningless to me. I assumed the book itself was not as wonderful as I had expected it to be. So I placed that book on a shelf, and it became part of my unread library.

A few years later, when I was looking for inspiration one evening, I was guided to open that book once again. This time, everything was different. The words within it now captivated my attention and spoke directly to my soul! They were inspiring me to see my world differently than I ever had.

What had changed? Logically, we must accept that the potential for ecstatic connection and heightened awareness was available to me when I first sat down to engage with this book. The book was absolutely the same in both moments. Only "I" had shifted the experience by naturally shifting my response and reaction to all that was presented in it.

Each element of our life perpetually serves as a force of inspiration and opportunity. But no element can ever hold essential power over our experience. What we encounter changes nothing—*until we react to it, respond to it, or participate with it in some way.*

All life works in this way.

Fresh juice can only be healthy for us if we believe that it's healthy for us; a loving relationship can only be real if we believe that it's loving; and a new dawn can only bring a fresh start if we believe that it does.

All reality exists in potential only, until we begin to shape it uniquely for our individual experience and journey.

This is why we can be considered the center of all creative life-force in our personal reality. We are the sole force that directs all primal energy forward in progressive motion for our own evolutionary growth and expansion.

"No outside force defines our reality."

~ **Divine Spirit**

For far too long we have believed that our experiences are shaped by our circumstances and our environment; but from the highest planes of divine understanding, that can never be. Even when we believe ourselves to be disempowered and without control, we have surrendered to that perception of truth in some way.

Ultimately, to "be disempowered" is still a choice within the full spectrum of choices that can be. Therefore, it is still an empowered act at some level of consciousness—and this is exactly where we must stretch our current understanding of Self.

It's entirely possible to be ignorant of our innate power at one level of awareness, while being fully aware of this power on another.

Each time that we believe ourselves to be limited in any way, we are focused upon that limited perception of truth as our only truth. In order to recognize our expanded aspects of Self, we must stretch our understanding of both what *is* and what *can be.*

Just like the witness to the building blueprint, we must acknowledge that there are other layers of design that exist beyond our current awareness. All perception of disempowerment is only a limited viewpoint of the greater all-encompassing truth. It must be, because upon alternate dimensions of understanding, we are always the center of all creative life-force.

We are always infinite in our potential!

As we learn to reclaim our *personal power* in our everyday lives, we begin to move the seat of power and awareness into our earthly consciousness. We begin to lift the veils of separation so that we intimately resonate with our divine nature and the infinite potential that already exists.

Essentially, we are blending the parts of us that "know" with the parts of us that have "forgotten." But regardless of where our focus rests in any particular moment, we must acknowledge that it's all part of who we eternally are.

For me, this is where my earthly persona feels triggered, and even a bit betrayed. Why was I never told that I am more than I imagine myself to be? Why was I never inspired to rise above my own limited thoughts and patterns? Why was I even encouraged to remain lost, confused, and alone through far too much of my experience?

If I have always been all that I eternally am, why could the wisest part of me not "save me" from all the sorrow I had known?

Even now, one part of me rises into acceptance of all higher awareness, while another part of me mourns all the lost moments that have been.

I still feel "abandoned" at deep levels of authentic being.

Perhaps you do too.

Do you sometimes feel disappointed in the world that surrounds you? Do you feel a bit wounded by the empty promises and challenged relationships that you may have been a part of? Do you feel unseen, unappreciated, and unloved?

If you do, this is exactly why we need to trust that only *we* can be the center of our own creative life-force. All shift and change must initiate itself from within.

We often place too much pressure and expectation upon the circumstances and relationships in our life. We instinctively know that we are looking for more than we are currently aware of, and then we believe that some other source—a relationship, opportunity, or belonging—holds the ability to heal that sense of lack within.

Yet, every time we expect to receive some form of acceptance, support, healing, peace, and security from an outside source, we are handing our power over to that potential source. We are trusting that they have something greater to offer than we hold within.

In doing this, we deny our own empowered path and surrender to the conditions of that external relationship. We forget that we, ourselves, are an ever-resourceful font of infinite potential and possibility.

We are the center of our own creative life-force and hold the ability to effortlessly attract all that might benefit and bless our own journey.

All my disappointment in life has come from believing that I was not supported and cared for. In each of those experiences, however, I was silently asking others to take responsibility for my own confident self-acceptance and security. I was believing that they could satisfy whatever sense of lack and loss had existed within me.

This is exactly why I was thrown into such a deep state of perceived loss in 2002.

If I had remained focused upon all that was a beautiful blessing in my own personal world, I would have moved through that pivotal moment with effortless grace. Instead, I was focused upon all that was happening around me—*outside of my direct control*—so I couldn't clearly see my empowered way through.

Despite all that dramatically unfolded in my life, nothing had shifted my core foundational truth; I was still the most brilliant, caring, wise, and masterful soul that I had always been. All that had shifted was how I saw myself.

I will share more about what triggered me into my own sense of loss a bit further on. But for now, the circumstances that pushed me into my own re-evaluation of Life aren't as important as the way I moved through them.

We each have our own purposeful stories of trauma, sorrow, and pain. My hope is to be a reminder that we are so much more than the experiences we've been a part of. We are not defined by those singular moments. We are defined by how we respond to them, one by one.

Everything had appeared overwhelming to me, in my own pivotal moment of change, because all that I had valued as a vital aspect of my personal identity was dependent upon that which existed outwardly. I held expectations for what would be, and when those expectations were shattered, I had no other foundation to stand on.

At the time, I couldn't yet understand that when our personal security—both emotionally and physically—is built upon expectations of identity and belonging, our peace and happiness is linked to the fulfillment of those expectations and assumptions.

In this respect, an "expectation" can be regarded as any means of measurement that we accept as viable and true. If we value and see our current roles, accomplishments, and identities as a measurement of our success and self-worth, then we are placing expectations upon ourselves to excel in these roles, accomplishments, and identities. However, if our personal identity is reliant upon the presence of any outward force or circumstance, then our purpose, value, and identity can be shattered, manipulated, or altered in any random and unexpected moment.

Let me explain that statement more clearly.

If we view our personal value in contrast to the presence or approval of an outside force, then our personal value can be impacted by that outside force's free-will choices. If we feel validated through the job we have, then we can potentially lose our sense of personal value if that job naturally evolves or transforms and is no longer there to support us.

Yet, if we recognize that the job is a form of beautiful support upon our greater journey of ever-present support and love, then we can still retain our strong sense of Self throughout any transition. When one source of support comes to a completion, we'll naturally redirect our focus to align with the next divine source of support.

The same can be said of a significant relationship. We can fully enjoy, honor, and celebrate the gift of a meaningful relationship without believing that the relationship is our foundation for a strong sense of Self. The relationship can inspire us, motivate us, and support us; but it does not hold the power to define us or place value upon our true and precious Self.

As we learn to see ourselves as our own *sacred source*, we open to the abundance that is ever-available.

Once we believe that all is possible, this world can bring through any number of supportive opportunities and experiences. We are never again bound to any single circumstance as our "source" of safety, security, and empowerment.

To remind myself of how infinitely supported I am, in any moments of challenge that might appear, I've learned to repeat this profound mantra to myself:

"I am my own sacred source."

This mantra keeps my focus within. It reminds me of just how powerful I am in creating my own reality. My life no longer has to spiral when something unexpected appears because I am able to stay grounded in my own foundation of immutable truth; I easily remember that my safety and security are constant and ever-present.

As the center of my own creative life-force, I am trusting that my every thought, prayer, and effort is placing energy into motion. This energy, at unseen levels, is calling out to all expressions of life that would comfortably support my experience. And it's this *energetic call* that attracts all opportunities and blessings into my life, with certainty.

I can focus upon being safe, for example, without attaching to any particular person, place, or circumstance as being "the source" of that safety. If it's not comfortable for one channel of potential support to assist me in any moment, another will appear.

In this way, what is best for us is just as important as what is best for others. For just as we are the center of our own creative life-force, so are they.

This is important to remember.

We often feel that the words or actions of another have the power to hurt us. But really, that soul is living their life according to their own perceptions of comfort and truth. We have to let them honor their own soul's guidance without any imposed expectations, conditions, or restraints.

Their journey is their own—and they can only support our journey when it's in harmony and alignment with their own.

We are speaking of a truly abundant reality—one where there is more than enough of everything for everyone, in all moments. Therefore, we can all find what we are uniquely searching for because there is always a greater *divine flow* actively bringing all into perfect balance, harmony, and alignment.

All that is required of us is to know what we wish to align with, energetically.

That is the key that we have to be clear about.

If we are focused upon our healthy intentions and desires, energetically, we are calling in the purest frequencies of love, truth, peace, joy, prosperity, freedom, and more. We are connecting to those energies that already exist and have an intimate relationship to us, as is stated in the second principle of masterful creation that we discussed earlier in this chapter.

However, in order to call these energies in with ease and grace, we must release any prejudiced perceptions of what these energies must look like.

If genuine love, truth, peace, joy, prosperity, or freedom appeared in your life, would you care what shape it took on? Would you be willing to lovingly let go of everything that did not energetically match those chosen frequencies, so that you could immerse yourself in the beauty of actually having all you desire?

This is the abundant world of infinite potential that we now step into.

I believe that we have been limiting our experiences according to that which we believed was possible—but as our awareness expands, so does our reality.

> *"You are divine frequency! When you begin to feel more elated, regardless of the experience, the world around you will begin to shed its old patterns of struggle and density too. If you want to live in peace, be peace. If you want to be respected, respect yourself. If you want to feel free in life, trust that you are free. Life is infinite in potentiality when we first make the brave effort to believe."*

~ Divine Spirit

We are intimately connected to so much more potential than we see. Life, as we know it, is as expansive as we allow it to be.

We are the channel through which all bold blessings find their form! *We are the center of our own creative life-force, and so much more.*

66

CHAPTER SIX

Perceptions of Self

"Allow your Spirit to BE in authenticity. Release every patterned behavior that encourages you to rationalize or validate who you are or should be. You are the prism of Light that inspires the sun to rise and the new day to dawn. Do not doubt the brilliance of your candid and uncensored truth. Your individuality is what brings much needed variation and free expression to this world."

~ Divine Spirit

Many of us have been indoctrinated to believe that we are a neat little compilation of chosen ideals, identities, and attributes. We easily describe ourselves as a loving child, a brave entrepreneur, a loyal companion, and a humble seeker—but these are all just stories we tell ourselves. They are reflections of the beliefs and the expectations we identify with in each passing moment.

As I delve more fully into my own self-discovery, I recognize that I can never genuinely be only that which I perceive myself to be. I am infinite in my potential and can easily shift my energy to resonate with countless points of truth upon any scale of free expression.

It's all me!

There will always be moments in which I treasure my sacred stillness, and moments in which I enjoy being the mindless jokester who finds comedy in every common detail of life. There will be moments in which I embody the wise peacemaker, and moments in which I stand strong as the uncompromising advocate for justice.

When your soul wishes to step beyond the bounds of your self-imposed limitations just a bit, are you gentle and kind with yourself?

Every unique form of free expression can essentially resonate and give voice to different parts of our boundless spirit. We don't need to carelessly deny any instinctual thought, emotion, or desire that might arise, because every unique facet of our intricate nature serves a purpose and conveys a message.

To embrace the emotion of sorrow does not mean that we need to entwine with it forever. We'll authentically process that emotion until we are ready to move forward to know laughter, joy, love, compassion, or any other precious emotion within the full spectrum of emotional being.

A creative artist does not fundamentally compromise their own integrity when they crave a bit of conformity and structure, and a trusted financier does not undermine their professionalism when they respectfully choose to act a bit child-like from time to time. As each of us learns to gracefully honor the instincts that rise from within, we become more comfortable in our own boundless nature, allowing ourselves to move through this dance called Life with much greater ease.

This was originally challenging for me to personally accept.

I had a very structured view of who I was and who I should be. I held myself to high expectations, and often judged myself harshly when I fell short of my intended ideal or goal. This also means that beneath the proud exterior, I was questioning my own purpose and worth. Without recognizing it, I was living in denial of my most beautiful and perfect *Authentic Self*.

During the early stages of my own awakening, my mind was often stuck in grief, and my emotions were sometimes pushed to the edge of what felt possible to endure. Life was changing for me, and waves of fear, loss, and sadness often guided my thoughts and awareness.

It was during one of these emotionally charged moments that my grief overtook me. The pain of loss filled me, and I couldn't see past the tears that flowed inconsolably. But, even in that innocent state of desperation, I still called out for support and love from all higher realms of divine being.

Quicker than my prayer could be expressed, I sensed my guides and guardians coming near. Their energy merged together as one sacred force to collectively echo:

"You're so beautiful!"

These words shocked me. They caused me to feel unseen and misunderstood. I was in the depth of sorrow and pain, with puffy eyes and tear-stained cheeks. How could I be considered "beautiful" by any stretch of the imagination?

With frustration in my voice, I asked *"Don't you see me?"*

They compassionately responded:

> *"Yes. Look at how brave you are, allowing yourself to authentically feel all that you feel."*

These words spoke to my soul and melted every perception of pain and sorrow that I had been holding onto. In that instantaneous moment, I understood the deeper meaning. *All potential truth is inherently beautiful!*

There is never anything to hide from or shield ourselves from because all facets of our intricate nature are perfect and pure in their most innocent form.

A beautiful force of Light had switched on from within, allowing me sight beyond that which was dense, heavy, and distracting. The perception that my pain was too overwhelming to bear was no more than an illusion.

I suddenly felt free—and I was ready to see clearly.

These bright guides and guardians reminded me that my ability to feel, emote, and passionately express myself only made me more beautiful. It was proof that my heart was open to all that was divine and sacred.

If I had not been feeling the depths of emotion I had felt, I would have been denying the experience. At some level, my spirit was aligning with the anguish and pain I already held within. In order to move beyond those valid emotions, I needed to honor that experience fully. I needed to feel it completely.

But when my soul was ready to grow and evolve beyond that anguish and pain, I innocently called out for support and inspiration. Without understanding what I required, my soul welcomed in all I was then ready to accept and receive.

It can be that easy.

Traditionally speaking, our society has created plenty of intimidating expectations for what is emotionally appropriate in each moment. These expectations have caused many of us to either suppress our emotions or to feel shame for all that we've expressed.

We carry a lot of wounds, personally and collectively, because of the arbitrary expectations that have been instilled into every generation. But these wounds are only surface deep. They can only remain as long as we identify with them.

When we are ready for new opportunities and viewpoints in our lives, our souls reach out for new inspiration. Even while we sometimes feel a bit lost and without direction, we continue to attract all that inspires us in new ways.

Our souls are intelligent expressions of pure life-force, connected to every other aspect of pure life-force. They always know how to masterfully guide us forward into new levels of conscious evolution.

I became stuck in the depth of my overwhelming emotions because I subconsciously judged them to be ugly, shameful, and painful in some way. I was giving them voice, but I was also allowing them to control me by considering that they had the ability to consume me. I honestly felt that my raw and candid expressions were something to hide and deny, as if my grief and sorrow marked me and made me unworthy.

Once my awareness was lifted, I began to see all emotion as beautiful. I was able to move purposely and powerfully through each stage of authentic emotional release. It was no longer "what I felt" that made my experience different. It was "how I looked at what I felt" that changed everything.

I learned to see through every shadowed perception—like doubt, insignificance, and fear—because these perceptions could never be the greatest truth.

Beyond the self-imposed veils of separation and limitation, I am all things. I am Light. I am Truth. I am Love.

71

And so are you.

> *"You are both Creator and Creation! You
> are the stars that illuminate all darkness
> and the earth beneath your feet. You are
> the cosmos unveiled and the butterfly in
> transformation. You are the breath you
> breathe and the eternity you journey
> through. You are all things. Do not doubt
> your Self today. You are the wonder we
> celebrate, in all ways."*

~ Divine Spirit

I didn't always see myself this way. I do now, because Spirit introduces this truth to me, with great compassion, patience, and tenacity. Every time my thoughts were less than inspiring, I heard the whispers of divine truth reminding me to look beyond all that felt so limiting and oppressive. I was being rebirthed, in a way, to see myself and all life through new sight.

This was the freedom that I had always yearned for, but never knew existed.

However, let's be honest. When these messages first started to flow naturally, I was still indoctrinated to fear everything that was unknown. I was doing my best to accept all that now felt empowering and uplifting, but I still had more questions than I did answers.

Blending these new truths with all that I had previously known was a challenging feat for someone who still needed to logically validate that this divine truth was "real."

Perhaps this *questioning* is even part of the initiation that every truth seeker must explore for themselves. I can certainly acknowledge that the act of questioning will always open new doors of awareness and understanding for one who is truly ready to see with new sight.

Here are some of the thoughts that were spiraling through my own curious mind:

- How does this "elevated truth" relate to the very physical world that I still live in?

- What do these greater insights say about the life I had lived up to that point?

- Is one perception of truth in natural conflict with another?

- Would I be betraying myself by shifting my beliefs so easily?

- Had I been living a lie up to that moment?

My mind was struggling to integrate all new and inspired understandings with that which had previously been. I suddenly found myself in a doorway of conscious evolution and spiritual transformation, wondering how all the varying viewpoints could possibly fit together.

As much as I was enjoying my newfound sense of freedom, I was also seeking validation for all that was shifting. If I was blinded to truth previously, how could I be certain that these new insights are worthy of my trust? All seemed a bit convoluted and nonsensical from this boundless state of conscious exploration.

I eventually found peace in accepting that this world is more intricate and complex than I can imagine.

Certainly, existence does not pause at my current level of awareness. Life has always expressed itself in more ways than I could perceive. All that was now unfolding for me, in extraordinary measure, was an expanded view of what had always been.

I was now being offered a sacred opportunity to see beyond the bounds of my own limited perceptions. All seemingly new insights were simply bringing alternate truths to the surface of my awareness.

> *"Accepting your divine nature need not shift that which appears to be real and true. Only your awareness shifts, to recognize that all which appears is not all that is."*
>
> ~ **Divine Spirit**

Every perception—each single point of view and understanding—exists independently from every other point of view and understanding. No expansion of our awareness can ever negate the power, purpose, and perfection of all that we've known in any other state of awareness.

I was only uncomfortable in my soul's growth because I had been trying to validate one experience in relation to the other. But if I could learn to see each experience as uniquely precious and purposeful, my anxiety would effortlessly transform into simple awareness.

If I could free myself from the ideals of structured conformity and expectation, I could relax into the freedom of *being present* in each new stage of soul growth and exploration.

A few years ago, one particular night was filled with incredibly uncomfortable dreams. Each dream scenario placed me in a parade of places, situations, and relationships that I then considered to be the exact opposite of my comfort zone.

In one dream, I found myself snowboarding down a mountainside with others who fully enjoyed it. In another, I was lost in what appeared to be a dangerous part of town. Scenario after scenario, the pain and discomfort continued.

When I woke in the morning, I asked my spirit guides why I would experience such a night. What could possibly be the purpose?

They showed me that when we are in vibrations that do not match our own, we feel uncomfortable. For instance, if we do not believe ourselves to be royal, then we would be uncomfortable in a royal palace. If we do not wish to drive fast, we would be uncomfortable in a race car.

Because we naturally align with the energies that support our current journey, there will always be countless energies that lie in opposition to those which make us comfortable. This doesn't make all opposing choices less than perfect; others might be profoundly blessed by that which doesn't feel personally supportive to us.

We all see the world from our unique perspectives, which can allow us to perceive all opposing interests and choices as less than perfect by comparison. But our *Divine Self* exists beyond all sense of contrast and opposition. It encourages us to see beauty and bravery in all unique forms of boundless life-expression.

From this enlightened awareness, all nuances of our intricate natures can be celebrated. We can learn to authentically love and accept every real, raw, and messy aspect of ourselves!

> *"No particular value can ever be placed upon the infinite nature we are, because 'infinite' by its nature is all-encompassing."*
>
> **~ Divine Spirit**

It's all beautiful. Every facet of authentic free-expression has its place and serves its purpose.

To remind myself that I never need to be any more than I am, I speak these words with power and focus:

> *"I love myself into wholeness!"*

All parts of me are needed for me to be "me."

I accept the fullness of all I am—*as I am.*

How about you?

CHAPTER SEVEN

Transcending Duality

"Imagine yourself as a Star, birthing itself into physicality and form without any concept of what came before. It would be easy to believe that all you see is all that is. But we ask you to delve deeper into your own sacred mysteries of truth. Can you recall the memories of being boundless Light and formless Spirit? This is you! Still. In all ways."

~ Divine Spirit

We are not our bodies, or even our logical minds. We are the boundless energy and spirit that flows through our physical forms and empowers everything we know.

We are the inconceivable, the miraculous, and the extraordinary. This is our truth!

Sometimes it's incredibly comfortable for me to accept this truth as absolute and unyielding, and sometimes I doubt it completely. Because a world of "duality" allows me to align with more than one viable truth, if I so choose, I can honestly identify with both our extraordinary natures and our limited personas.

We are all part of this curious dynamic. In a reality of duality, we can genuinely identify with more than one independent frequency and perspective within the full spectrum of potentiality.

We can fully trust that we're loved and supported in one moment, and then authentically question whether we're loved and supported in the next. We can see ourselves as the champion of our own personal journey, and we can also remain in fear of the unknown path that lies ahead.

> *"Walking through the haze-filled edge of time between time, plane between plane, and reality between reality, you are reminded that it's all within your scope of authentic beingness. Never are you detached from one or the other. It's only your focused energy and intention that allows you to identify with one over the other."*

> ~ **Divine Spirit**

In learning to transcend our duality, we learn to live consciously, with clear sight. We learn to disempower that which merely *appears* to hold truth on the surface, so that we may reach deeper within ourselves for greater discernment and inspiration.

But duality isn't the only phenomenon that we need to transcend in order to consciously rise. There is also the issue of *forgetfulness*, which subtly distracts us from our greatest truth.

Forgetfulness is an inherent aspect of duality. It implies that we have all the information that we might possibly need, without acknowledging that there is always more than can be seen. It is the quintessential understanding of "not knowing what we don't know."

Can we agree that much of humanity is currently lost within the swoon of forgetfulness?

It's not judgment when I say this. I include myself in this delusionary view of reality. Seeing clearly, without false perception, is something I continue to strive for.

I mention this now because it's important to know that we are never stepping into new and impersonal aspects of ourselves when we expand our current awareness. We are merely awakening the dormant memory of all that we authentically are, beyond the veil of forgetfulness and separation.

We are divine Light, embodied in human form. But in a reality of duality and separation, that Light is not always apparent. It's often cloaked by the appearance of physicality, structure, and conformity. It's up to us to look deeper—*beyond than that which appears*—so that we might learn to trust that which we discern as true for ourselves.

As a society, we have been indoctrinated to accept all that is physical, factual, verifiable, and tangible as our only source of potential reality. But, as one who is awakening from the slumber of forgetfulness, it's important to remember that there are infinite realms of truth that lie beyond those logical planes of awareness.

All realities, including those that are currently unseen, are part of our authentic experience. They all co-exist with our own reality and are available to support our journey as needed.

Although living in a world of duality can easily encourage us to perceive one experience as better than or less than another, it does not impose any reality upon us as a certain and uncompromising condition. It only offers us an opportunity to resonate with all forms of opposition, limitation, imperfection, and separation, if we so choose.

All is still a choice.

That choice is what directly shapes our reality and allows us to intentionally reclaim connection to our *empowered* and *sovereign beingness.* It's how we learn to express ourselves freely, to gracefully explore all potential realities.

So, in trusting that there is a great variety of choice always available to us, how do we become comfortable in making wise choices for ourselves? Especially if we've been doing our best to avoid decision-making up until this point.

Many of us have been following paths that were laid out for us, while denying our secret desires to make independent choices for ourselves. Even in the smallest of ways, we've been surrendering our privileged right to choose our own reality.

We accept that our body will be hungry at midday, before we ever move through our day with objectivity; we believe that unexpected traffic will make us late for an appointment, without ever considering that all can easily balance itself out; and we envision that broken glass will be troublesome to clean up, before we've even tried to do so.

In each of these experiences, we've applied our past perceptions to our current situation, thereby surrendering our sovereign right to choose consciously and creatively in each present moment.

We can, however, intentionally shift our everyday experiences by expanding our point of view. We can bravely look beyond all that appears to be our only viable choices, to discern what other options and possibilities might be available to us.

In truth, we only need to shift one little element for our whole experience to authentically shift.

Our choice to act, or to not act, in any particular way changes the experience. *Every single time, both our effort and our non-effort make a difference.*

When we remember this, we begin to see ourselves as the catalyst of potential shift and change. We begin to see ourselves as the empowered ones—always in control of our personal experiences.

No matter how many infinite choices may appear, it's always *our choice* that shapes our destiny.

We only become lost and bewildered in the dualistic experience when we have lost connection to our own inner voice and guidance. By learning to transcend duality, we begin to trust and value our own insights, instincts, and choices above all others. We begin to access higher truth for ourselves, and to look within for direct guidance and clarity.

Within the chasms of our unexplored Self lies all wisdom, truth, knowledge, and inspiration. Within the limitless expanse of our own truest nature, we always know what is best for our unique journey.

The appearance of duality, in this earth-based reality, is no more than a distraction to tempt us away from our wise, all-knowing Self. And that is as it should be, because even this realm of illusion is purposeful when seeking to discover our truest nature. When we finally become disillusioned with all that surrounds us outwardly, we begin to purposefully delve into the unexplored recesses within our own precious Self.

A few years ago, my family and I were exploring the wilderness of Maine on ATV's. Without recognizing it, we had ventured into unmaintained paths that were extremely challenging (even a bit traumatic) to navigate. By the time we reached our destination, we had become concerned about making it back to our starting point before dark.

We decided that my cousin, as the strongest and boldest driver, would take one ATV back to the starting point and then come back to retrieve us in a "real" vehicle that could navigate public roads.

When my beautiful 12-year old son asked if he could go with him, I said "Yes" without thinking. My first instinct was to not hold him back from an adventure; but as soon as they left, my heart fell to the ground. I couldn't take a deep breath! I had suddenly realized they were heading back into that "dangerous wilderness" where anything could happen.

The thoughts of having no phone reception, no food, and no other traffic on that unmaintained path were swirling dramatically inside my head. I couldn't see past the irrational fears and insecurities that were unexpectedly triggered.

In that state of authentic panic, I asked Spirit to be with me.

Before my prayer was complete, I felt a divine touch wash through me, bringing peace and calm. It miraculously healed every sense of fear and insecurity. In fact, I could no longer force myself to doubt my son's safety. I was confident in knowing that they would be back in perfect time—and they were.

This story illustrates the profound difference that two contrasting points of view can make in our lives.

My son was physically safe when he left, but I chose to align with perceptions of limitation and lack. I could have remained in that choice for as long as I wished, but when I was ready to accept a different perspective, I asked for higher truth to be with me.

I didn't ask for my son's safety; I asked for greater truth. I asked to rise beyond the perception that my son could be unsafe.

This is why, I believe, peace filled me so completely. I had connected to an authentic truth that already existed upon a higher plane of consciousness. If I had prayed for his safety, I would have been energizing the belief that he could be unsafe. I still would have been participating in an experience of duality—where "safe or unsafe" was a possibility.

By asking for divine support, I asked to rise beyond all illusion, so that I might transcend the perception of duality in that moment. Duality was still present and available because it was still a choice to believe in challenge or security. But I had asked for the highest truth, and miraculously found my way through.

Our souls, individually and collectively, are already programmed and encoded to instinctively reach towards greater understandings of truth—especially in times of confusion and fear.

With each sacred step, we move closer into union with the divine and all infinite planes of loving support. We remember that we are not alone!

The perception that we are limited and small, by comparison, is illusion.

> *"No moment, no potentiality, no essence of being, or perception of truth can exist outside of your truest Self. It's all an intricate and infinite aspect of You."*

> **~ Divine Spirit**

We're all learning to trust in this infinite aspect of our Self because, ironically, we still hold onto the belief that "struggle and lack" is an inherent aspect of this earthly existence.

We have never learned to accept our experiences of struggle and lack as mere choices in the full spectrum of infinite choice. They are always present, as an option, but they hold no more power or influence than joy and love do.

A few years ago, I had another amazing night of dream teachings that elevated my understanding of contrast, contradiction, and duality. The dream scenarios shifted and changed throughout the night, but in each one, I was always challenged by some great obstacle or distraction.

Although I came through each momentary struggle victoriously, I grew more and more tired of the greater "challenge" that was ever flowing. It seemed that every victory was only fleeting because there was always another challenging scenario to break my peaceful state of triumphant being.

Does this perception of endless struggle sound familiar to you? I have often felt this way, and I don't believe I'm the only one.

In the last dream scenario of that challenging night, all sense of normal reality suddenly fell away. An open field of wild grass appeared before me, and a sacred tree with an unearthly radiance captured my attention. This great tree represented the perfect union of two seemingly opposing forms of life. It appeared as though the trunk of a pure black tree, dark as night, had gracefully entwined itself with the trunk of a pure white tree, luminous in every way.

I witnessed the contrast of their two distinct energies with my physical sight, but on a deeper level I knew that to give attention to only one half of the whole would be meaningless. *The beauty of one could not be honored and treasured without the complementing beauty of the other.*

They were two aspects of one radiant life-force, supporting each other in their own respective wholeness.

I clearly understood that, entwined as they were, one could not exist without the presence of the other. Each one brought balance and purposeful reflection to the other's light.

This tree was teaching me to celebrate the variation of all expansive life expression, without encouraging me to see "variation" as intrinsically separate.

Each unique aspect of the One plays a vital and purposeful role within the whole. In this perfect union, all sense of comparison and arbitrary contrast fades away. We learn to recognize that each is intrinsically beautiful in its own unique way.

> *"When Black and White vie as One, Peace will come again."*
>
> **~ Divine Spirit**
> **Through a Dream Teaching**

These words repeated themselves over and over as I absorbed the full understanding of all they conveyed.

We are learning to release from the belief that either black or white, rich or poor, young or old, divine or human, can be better than its contrasting partner. Each is a sacred expression of the single and all-encompassing whole. *Each is purposeful in its own way.*

When assumed values no longer have a place in our society, peace will come again. The only separation that can be is that which we perceive!

And so, from this point of acceptance and understanding, the long enduring battle between right and wrong can begin to lovingly transcend to a heightened space of nonjudgment and grace.

> *"When stepping into sacred remembrance, it's important to reclaim your personal power to the highest degree. All parts of your authentic nature contribute to the miracle that is you. They all bring contrast, balance, and harmony to the whole. All parts of you are precious, and worthy of love."*

> **~ Divine Spirit**

It's time to honor each unique expression of our boundless spirit as *perfect* and *pristine*.

Duality only offers an abundance of choice upon our journey. It never holds us back from being all we wish to be.

CHAPTER EIGHT

Nonjudgment as a Path

"Let go of the ideal! We cannot discover our own empowered potential unless we step out of all limited structure, perceived and physical."

~ Osiris

This precious Life is one of ever-spiraling possibility and potential. There will never be only one ideal way to honor every soul, every moment, and every purposeful intention that is or can be. Infinite and boundless expression will always be a precious aspect of our reality.

What is now shifting, fundamentally, is our subjective interpretation of each boundless expression that is. One soul's *personal choice* has no direct impact upon, or relevance towards, any other soul's choice.

Individuality is always a gift.

One way is no greater than any other.

Climbing Mt. Everest holds no greater intrinsic value than does teaching children in San Francisco to read. Essentially, there is no need to compare. Each experience naturally holds its own set of unique virtues and values without needing to be compared to the other. The brave soul who chooses to climb Mt. Everest may feel completely out of place in a San Francisco classroom.

In other words, what is natural to one bright soul, may be incredibly foreign and uncomfortable to another.

We can never assume to know what is best for another precious soul—*or to even imagine the intricacies of their unique life journey.* All forms of assumption must gently dissipate if we are to look at our world through the eyes of compassionate nonjudgment and love.

And it might actually require a moment of patient transition before we can truly see ourselves and others through a lens of pure acceptance. This space of integration is often necessary because our minds have been indoctrinated to view everything in comparison to some standard of arbitrary appropriateness.

The purest concept of "nonjudgment" is not yet an understanding that we are intimately familiar with.

As children, we learned that a clean room was better than a messy room, that eating vegetables was better than eating cookies, and that passing an exam was better than failing. These conditions may have positively served particular moments in our life, but if they are carried forward into all fresh, new moments without conscious awareness, they become assumptions.

Every soul is following its heart's guidance, and we must allow each soul responsibility for their own precious experiences. Of course, like many things, this can be easier said than done.

I completely agree with this, logically. But I struggled to accept it in regard to some real-world situations. How could

I watch others stumble and fall, in my shallow opinion, without helping them?

If I am a "good" person, shouldn't I save people from their challenged path?

That used to be my belief system.

I couldn't see, at first, how judgmental that concept truly is.

I couldn't stretch beyond the perception of what is "right and wrong" because it was all I ever knew. It shaped the way I looked at everything in my life, including my own choices and decisions.

In fact, when I first began introducing nonjudgment into my world, I could only relate it to nonjudgment of others. I couldn't yet apply it to my own experiences because I had built up blinders to all that was personal for me.

Accepting my own "wrong" choices was too painful to think about.

In order to heal myself, and my false perceptions of judgment and righteousness, I had to begin outwardly. I focused on shifting the original programming that taught me to see *others* as helpless victims.

Ultimately, it wasn't to bring healing to them, it was to bring healing to myself. I simply needed to direct my attention outwardly because it was more comfortable for me to see others as "right or wrong" than it was for me to see myself.

It might be the same for you.

But as long as I presumed anyone to be in a state of need or distress, I was feeding a perception of challenge and struggle. It was time for me to see each soul as empowered and resourceful, regardless of that which appeared to be true.

I finally understood this sacred teaching more fully thanks to a sweet little turtle that crossed my path one day.

While driving, I spotted this turtle in the middle of a road, quite near my home. I didn't hesitate to pull over and attempt to save his little turtle life, as I had done for several other turtles before. But as I reached down to embrace this innocent one, Spirit's voice echoed in my ear, saying, *"Who are you to know what is best for this turtle?"*

I suddenly sensed that my desire to "save him" was incredibly self-righteous and ignorant. I wasn't acting upon intuitive guidance or irresistible instinct. I simply assumed that this turtle was lost, alone, and incapable of supporting itself. What gave me the right to label him as a victim? My assistance may have redirected him from his soul's journey and purpose.

With this new awareness, I chose to return to my car and say a prayer for him and his safety instead. But Spirit then told me that it would be just as judgmental to assume that every turtle I would ever encounter in the middle of a road would not require assistance as well.

We must learn to approach each life experience from a nonjudgmental heart space. Only then can we tune into what might authentically be needed in each moment, without prejudice.

I had, before that day, assumed that turtles were without power in their lives. However indirectly I had originally adopted this belief, it had become an accepted truth in my reality. I had not even paused to imagine that it might be otherwise.

Spirit used this lesson to seed a much greater teaching into my awareness. Ultimately, they were reminding me that if I held prejudiced assumptions for this innocent turtle, it might be possible that I held prejudiced assumptions for many other forms of life.

> *"Do not doubt! Each soul knows the path they must walk. They know, better than anyone, the twists and the turns that will lead them home. Cheer them on! Remind them that they are not alone. But do not, with all your best intentions, interfere in the path that they must walk. They wish to discover how extraordinary they are."*

> ~ **Divine Spirit**

Every soul is connected to their own limitless source of internal wisdom, guidance, and inspiration. Whether they are aware of these divine resources or not, they are present and available. *Always.*

We can all acknowledge that perceptions of victimhood, struggle, and conflict are intricately woven into our current belief systems. But they do not represent our greatest truth. *They are only perceptions of truth that can easily shift with conscious intent when we are ready.*

To do this, we must first understand that we have adopted these perceptions through indoctrinated patterning. At some point, in timeless being, we have believed the stories that have been told. We believed that we could be victims to unjust circumstances. We believed that we should be warriors in a battle for rights that are already ours to claim. We believed that we could be disempowered in a world of disorder and disharmony.

But these beliefs keep us bound to the limited perceptions of an unsafe world.

As an example, many of us still feel a need to survive and to prove our self-worth because we were once taught to accept these behaviors as normal and acceptable. We were trained to attain success, property, respect, and even love—and then we were simultaneously taught that all we achieved and attained could be taken from us if we were not careful.

So, each step forward became entwined with the belief that we must defend, protect, and preserve all that is ours.

This desire to protect "what is ours" can be applied to our health, our wealth, our reputation, our possessions, and our relationships. From an individual point of view, it can speak of our personal worlds. From a grander, macrocosmic point of view, it can speak of our communities, societies, and nations.

It's all the same.

We process much of our life and our experience from a survival mentality. We see ourselves, and every other incarnate soul, as either the victor or the victim.

But, by learning to transcend our duality, we step into *the victimless path*—which accepts that there are no victims in life. There are only participants, choosing the energies, frequencies, vibrations, and patterns that best support their own unique journey.

Some of us are very sensitive about the word "victim." So, let's shift our understanding to simply symbolize one who feels *disempowered* and *without choice*. This relates to even the smallest perceptions of disempowerment, including every time a bully has told us to be quiet, every time we believed that something was lost, and every time we held ourselves back from doing something we love.

Many of us have become so entwined in patterns of insignificance and disempowerment that we have forgotten how exceedingly remarkable we are. We have forgotten how to trust our own empowered instincts that know how to push us beyond each false perception and limited truth that no longer serves.

What we often regard as a "challenge" is merely an opportunity to reprogram the old and outdated patterns that once resonated. In those moments of discomfort, we consider whether we are ready to now see the patterns of disempowerment differently than we once did.

In truth, we wouldn't have attracted that perception of momentary confusion, chaos, or conflict unless we originally resonated with its energy. And we won't be able to thoroughly clear it until we see ourselves detaching from it and freeing ourselves from its embrace.

Every challenge offers us an opportunity to rise beyond all that we once accepted as an inflexible reality. When we are ready to stretch our perception of what can be, everything changes.

> *"You may wish to see yourself at the top of this evolutionary ladder of growth, but that will never be. Your journey will always continue further, to explore even greater awareness than you have known. So, you see, the end is not your destination! The journey is what you truly seek. Each moment leads you into greater self-discovery."*
>
> **~ Divine Spirit**

Each soul, consciously or subconsciously, designs its own experience with every thought, action, and choice they make.

They innately know what is needed to push them forward upon their own path into sacred empowerment and self-love.

In fact, every soul is the sovereign architect of their own inspired destiny, as we discussed earlier.

Accepting this enlightened understanding is one of my greatest lessons in this lifetime. As early in life as I can recall, I witnessed the pain and struggle that this earth-experience can bring to others. I sensed their fear, their perceived frailty, and their lack of self-confidence. I was focused upon seeing them as helpless and disempowered—*so that was all I saw.*

In response, I became the warrior, the savior, and the wise one willing to support their journey. I entwined my own uncertain perception of Self into all that would honor and benefit their experience, without a conscious understanding of how it would affect my own. I essentially became a martyr for the "greater good," because I did not yet know how to see everything through nonjudgment and love.

Although my intentions were pure, my choices were feeding the perceptions of lack and limitation. I was motivated by fear, not love. I was empowering no one.

> *"There are no victims. There are only participants."*
>
> **~ Divine Spirit**

To help me recognize how ancient my alignment with victimhood and struggle was, I was gifted with a profound past life vision, one day.

In this vision, my first intense and passionate awareness was of myself clutching a massive gash in my abdomen. I was collapsed against a pile of debris. I saw only devastation and destruction in all directions. I witnessed neighbors fighting neighbors, and I saw blood flowing like a river down the crevices of a cobblestone road. The sound of endless chaos was booming in my ears.

I had incarnated into the French Revolution.

I saw myself as a 22-year old boy who had tried incessantly to be a voice of peace and truth in a society that was setting itself to inevitably implode. I felt alone and unseen on that unsuccessful journey.

Feeling deeply connected to that ancient part of myself, I could scan through those 22 years of physical life and see that I was quietly dismissed and disregarded, never being viewed as a purposeful entity in that society. Even at the end of that life, I stood on the sidelines, unintentionally hit by shrapnel from a nearby explosion. I died alone and unseen on a pile of debris.

At the time, I had grown accustomed to visions like this one. I could journey through each moment as if I were living the experience directly. I was able to smell the smoke and feel the sweat mixed with dirt upon my skin. Every sensation was clear and intensified, bringing deeper understanding to the bigger picture.

In this particular vision, I felt no emotional pain for myself or my situation in that life-experience. I felt only the pain of witnessing humanity choosing self-righteous devastation over compassionate creation.

I knew that discomfort and pain well. I have been feeling it through much of my current life. Even now, I am still able to align with it if I am not cautious and aware.

In my work with countless clients over the years, I can also acknowledge that this is a trait that many conscious and awakening souls have in common. We innately know that peace is a potential reality, so we interpret non-peace as a painful experience.

In doing so, however, we feed this shallow perception.

In the life I just shared with you, I was fruitless in my endeavors to enlighten and inspire because I had perceived that there was a better way to be. I had made great efforts to continuously push my own beliefs and ideals on to others, without truly respecting their unique journeys.

At the end of that past life vision, I was able to watch that aspect of myself re-unite with my *Divine Self* upon the heavenly planes of consciousness. I witnessed a graceful merging, between the parts of me that were lost in illusion and the parts of me that knew only love.

From this heightened point of awareness and clear sight, the disappointment and pain disappeared. It melted away in the love that was eternal and all-encompassing.

I was then able to look upon that entire earthly experience as a non-emotional witness and clearly see that I was never meant to change another in any way.

I chose to participate in that incarnation because I still held onto the belief that humanity was blind to their greater potential, and I would not be able to elevate that limited belief until I explored other ways of looking at it.

That lifetime provided me an opportunity to discover how shallow and misguided my original beliefs were. Although my intentions were innocent and pure, my motivations were founded in fear and lack. I was participating in perceptions of victimhood (regarding others) and righteous martyrdom (regarding myself).

It was time for those perceptions to shift.

"All lifetimes provide an opportunity to discover your own boundless nature. Sometimes you incarnate so that you might discover all you are. But sometimes you incarnate so that you might discover all that you are not. You come to heal the perceptions of limitation and lack. Do not see your experience as a reflection of 'who you are.' It is merely a reflection of who you believe yourself to be.

When you are ready to know only love— you will know only love."

~ Divine Spirit

We all incarnate into particular lifetimes so that we may further our soul's understanding of what can be. We come to experience, to express, and to create freely, without bounds or constraints. It all leads us to higher perception, truth, and understanding.

There are no victims.

There are only participants.

CHAPTER NINE

Human Nature

*"We didn't incarnate so that we would
forget who we are. We incarnated into this
beautiful earthly form so that we could
discover who we are. This is why we
breathe, we step forward, we trust in the
happy ending, and we reach for the stars.
It's all part of a great big timeless desire to
know ourselves!"*

~ Divine Spirit

In our evolution towards higher consciousness, it is vital to
move past any assumption which implies that "being human"
is intrinsically less miraculous than being divine. If we see our
human nature—our core foundational truth—as limited in
any way, then we shall never be able to embrace our *Divine
Self* upon this earth plane.

We, as a human collective, were originally birthed in love. We
lived in harmony and peace for many earth cycles, and still
hold that remembrance within.

The patterns of defense, greed, conflict, and disharmony that
are so rampant across the earth plane at this time are not
"natural" to our enlightened selves. *They are learned and
adopted patterns of behavior that became rooted in times of
chaos and confusion.*

The surest way to neutralize these limiting patterns and beliefs is to cultivate a strong sense of self-awareness, individually and collectively.

It's time to remember who we are.

Let's first dispel any belief that implies we must restrain our human nature in order to be part of a civilized society. That is nonsense and teaches us to limit our authentic truth! Our true human nature is always extraordinary and infinite. It's an expression of our divine nature, in human form.

Our humanity allows space for each unique and individual soul to express themselves without bounds or defined structure. It honors the differences between each precious spirit and allows for each soul's unseen instinctual nature to be a valid source of guidance and direction.

True *human nature* is miraculous and beautiful, holding no expectation or judgment for what should be.

The appearance of anything less than miraculous and beautiful is only a limited perception of the greater truth.

Throughout time, there have been those who have diminished and demonized the beauty of our free will and our human nature in efforts to easily control the behavior of the populace. Unless our choices, beliefs, and actions were in alignment with the controlling faction of the day, we were made to feel inadequate, unworthy, separate, and alone on our journey to *understand* and *value* ourselves.

We have all been part of these limiting experiences in the past, and we can still recognize their impacts on our belief systems today. *Those experiences of struggle, abuse, betrayal, and abandonment are real within that level of conscious awareness, but they do not inherently represent our human nature!*

Human experience is not intrinsically dense and filled with struggle. The belief that it is so is founded in illusion.

All elements of chaos and confusion that exist upon the earth plane have been introduced and embraced by free-will choice. Their continued presence in our life is due to our continued alignment with their presence, even in the subtlest of ways.

By reclaiming a heightened understanding of what is natural and instinctual to humanity, we can begin to free ourselves from the limited perceptions and paradigms we have previously embraced. It is only when we believe ourselves to be "only human" that we intrinsically limit our infinite nature from expressing itself freely.

We are not "only human." We are infinite expressions of divine Light, having a human experience.

So, let's ponder upon what a human experience is.

Each innocent soul is originally born into this physical experience so that it can sense and discover the beauty that it is as a sovereign essence of ever-flowing divinity. It wishes to sense how its own unique Light affects and influences the universal whole. But how does this innocent soul explore its own individuality if it can only recognize itself as a merged aspect of the all-encompassing One?

For individual exploration and growth, some sense of separation must take place.

Individuality allows our *Divine Selves* to imagine, dream, and create as independent entities by forming a contrast between ourselves and the world around us.

> *"It's no great feat to be Light in the midst of only Light."*

> ~ **Divine Spirit**

The only way we can discover our own potentiality, as an individual or as a universal force, is to consciously step free from the previous parameters we have known.

This doesn't mean that we fundamentally change our core essence, truth, and nature in order to step into a new experience; it only means that we allow our brightest soul aspect, our *Divine Self*, to be birthed into a new experience for the purpose of limitless self-discovery.

In this case, we're talking about birthing our *Divine Self* into a human experience.

An innate part of that human experience is the presence of illusion and false perception. This illusion, however, is not designed to deceive us. It's designed to empower us. We still remain a pure and pristine aspect of the One, despite all appearances to the contrary.

The cloak of separation and limitation that we often give credence to, from our human perspective, is only a chosen state of being. *It is thought consciousness manifest!*

Therefore, we can just as easily create and manifest a positive human experience by bringing our divine nature and free spirit into our thought consciousness daily.

All veils of separation and illusion will naturally lift when our thoughts are focused upon our infinite potential, ability, and free-will choice.

> *"I watched you breathe yourself into creation, simply because you wished to love fully, in all ways. You did not ask for the 'easy' path. You asked to love fully, in all ways. This is still your soul's greatest purpose and desire. Look through the shadows that appear so imposing. For even they cry out to know love fully, in all ways.*

You are the embodiment of all that teaches, radiates, and awakens love fully, in all ways. Be yourself without fear and regret. You are the heart of all that is love, fully, in all ways. "

~ **Lord Melchizedek**

Our nature is to love and inspire; to see light in the shadows and hope in the darkness. Do not believe that you are lost or without direction! You are here to love fully, in all ways. Let that instinctual encoding find expression in every experience that you know.

As easily as we say "hello" to someone who gently approaches, deep wisdom can rise from within. It's natural for our soul to give expression to that which is intuitively sourced. The remembrance of knowing all things upon divine planes of awareness lies within our instinctual nature—*and it is looking for a voice.* By trusting these timeless insights to rise, without censor, we welcome divine consciousness into our human experience.

When I first considered stepping onto a path of teaching, sharing, and lighting the way, I had great difficulty trusting that I had enough wisdom and insight to share with others. Who was "I" to light the way?

In those moments of original doubt, I was only looking through the eyes of insignificance, separation, and fear. Those were the patterned responses I had been programmed to believe when faced with any offers of greatness and beauty. They were the old, soon-to-be obsolete, beliefs of a constrictive paradigm and society.

Once I accepted that I am always clearly connected to universal source, I found peace within. There could never be any information, knowledge, or truth that I could be separate from, so long as my heart remains open to receive from the infinite flow.

It was my pure intention and heart-centered intuitive knowing that would allow me to be all that I wished to be in each consecutive moment. I didn't need to acquire greater measures of conventional knowledge in order to be of genuine service and support to my community.

I only needed to believe that "I am enough."

Once I no longer resisted the divine wisdom and truth that effortlessly rose from within, I became an incredibly clear channel. Without recognizing it, I had shifted my personal point of power and focus towards the bright unseen Spirit within my Self. I silently gave permission for all universal Light to move through me, and it changed the way I saw everything.

Are you ready for that level of divine connection within your own Self too?

Imagine a world that instantly responds to your every inquiry and need. One that dances with you, as you navigate through every unexpected twist and turn. Never would you feel alone, incapable, or without control.

As authentic truth seekers, we are all on a journey of collective awakening. We are learning to trust our intuition, innate wisdom, and creative capacities in greater measure each day. And this expansion of human consciousness is reaching far beyond our "individual needs."

As we progressively feel more empowered within our own skins, we begin to passionately inspire our families and our communities too. We begin to acknowledge that there is an unseen interconnected web of Life, and that each one of us is vitally important to the whole.

"Each of us, in our own way, has been tasked with spreading the seeds of knowledge and truth in this life. Some of us will spread these seeds by being examples upon our own paths. We will step bravely into the unknown and bring greater connection and acceptance to new ideas, beliefs, and paradigms. We open the doors to fresh insight and untapped potential. We look past the fear and doubt, to dance joyfully in the realms of free expression and soul exploration. We are the dreamers who feel our way through each step upon the journey. We trust our natural instincts to guide the way."

~ **Divine Spirit**

Society has encouraged us to sometimes believe that our human nature is violent, selfish, and greedy, but there is nothing natural about those traits and characteristics. Those shallow, fear-based attributes are *learned characteristics* that no longer resonate with those of us who choose a loving approach to life.

We are sacred beings, created in Love—which we are now clarifying as the embodiment of "all-encompassing acceptance." *Without compromise, our nature is to passionately love and be loved.*

All other perceptions of "natural traits" are adopted behaviors that have only become natural to us. They will remain constant in our lives for as long as we accept them, but they are inherently subjective and changeable. Our only constant and immutable traits are those that are innately divine— united in wholeness and founded in Love.

Spirit tells me that we are learning to see ourselves as *earthly divine*—which is a gentle way of saying that we are "divinity incarnate."

All perceptions of limitation, separation, and lack are but remnants of ancient fear and doubt. They are the tethers of a conflicted mind; one that wants to be free but doesn't believe it can be. By embracing our true human nature (that which is divinely attuned), we break free of those illusionary binds to become our own sovereign authority.

CHAPTER TEN

Free-Will Choice

"See yourself in wholeness, as Life itself.
See yourself as the Peace you wish to know,
the Love you wish to embody, and the Joy
you wish to embrace. Become that which
you wish to Be—by will."

~ Divine Spirit

For humanity to gracefully rise from the mire of its programmed existence, we must bring greater understanding to the ethics and concepts of *personal responsibility* and *personal truth*.

We have all, in some way, blindly accepted a large number of "truths" without discerning whether they had any resonance with us personally. We have surrendered our empowered voice by assuming that all *implied truth* held the same value and significance as *personal truth*.

This dynamic is now progressively changing because we are learning to value our own sacred voices above all others.

Those around us, even those with the very best of intentions, can only "presume to know" that which we have the ability to confidently know for ourselves. This doesn't mean that we need to close ourselves off to the guidance and advice that they may offer. They may actually be seeing something that we have yet to see for ourselves, from an inspired point of view.

I am only suggesting that we generously accept the inspiration that others offer, *without ever diminishing the power of our own internal guidance*. In truth, we are the only ones who can possibly discern, with natural instinct and intuitive ability, that which is undeniably best for ourselves.

And for a purposeful moment, I'd like to place a bit of extra attention upon the words "for ourselves." We have been subliminally taught that placing attention upon ourselves is often selfish and egotistical. But this fundamental mistruth must now be compassionately healed.

If we are not living for our Self, who should we be living for?

Without any sense of shame, we have the right to make ourselves—and all that benefits us—a priority! There is always a respectful way to do this without placing any sense of lack or limitation upon another.

This is an important distinction to make. The concept of "selfishness" has been greatly distorted over time. As a fact, it only means that one is devoted to one's self. But as a society, we have accepted it to mean that we are consuming some vital life-force that might otherwise be directed elsewhere.

We have innocently believed that our own abundance can inherently diminish the abundance of another.

How absurd!

If we are all empowered and infinite within our potential, how can that possibly be true?

In this abundant world in which we live, there is more than enough of everything for everyone. I mentioned this earlier, but it's definitely important enough to mention again. *We can each live as abundantly as we choose, without ever diminishing that which is available to the whole.*

Our intentional choices—to accept, receive, and welcome all that we are worthy of—are what allow us to wield power over our everyday experiences. We can never give up the right to choose! It's how we secure the blessed and abundant path for ourselves.

In fact, creating an abundant reality can only become complex and overwhelming when we believe that there is opposition to all that we are worthy of.

Our choices effortlessly place energy into motion, but if we believe that our personal world is somehow in competition and conflict with the expansive world that exists outwardly, we will hold ourselves back from making the bold choices that allow us to experience life fully.

Can you identify with this limiting belief?

Many of us have been living this way because we have forgotten the *potential* and *power* that we naturally wield. We often surrender to the many distractions that redirect us from our own empowered path. But it is now time to remember this; only we have direct influence over our unique and precious experiences.

To bring greater clarity to this teaching, we must acknowledge the profound difference between *our world* and *the world*. One speaks of all that fills our immediate perceptions of what is and what can be. It's personal and unique to our individual journey. The other offers full potential and possibility for all life forms, and can never be only that which supports the benefit of a few.

It will always represent all things.

In recognizing that our world is custom-designed to match all that honors our unique journey, we accept that we do not ever need to fit into any environment that is overwhelming or uncomfortable. Everything can exist outwardly—as an opportunity for those who would be blessed—without it ever being part of our personal reality.

Essentially, we are accepting that everything is possible within the full spectrum of infinite possibility, but none of it is imposed upon us by circumstance alone. There is always an element of *free-will choice* that allows us to participate, or not participate, in each potential outcome that presents itself.

The intimate world of our personal awareness is subject to only that which we choose to co-create with.

And whether we see our world as small and contained, or as infinite and expansive, the same truth applies. Only we, through discernment and choice, have the power to impact and shape our personal world, i.e., our personal realities.

All we recognize as part of our reality is a reflection of all that we personally hold to be relevant and true.

Growing up, my father was insistent upon telling me, quite regularly, *"That's not reality! That's not the way the world works."* It didn't matter what the topic of discussion was. As long as my thoughts differed from his, he sought to impose his restrictive views of a single, uncompromising existential reality upon me.

Although, at the time, I had not yet understood that all realities are subjective to the individual, there was always a part of me that defied his confident declarations. I innocently knew that he just didn't know what he didn't know.

My father had learned to see his world through a black-and-white lens of right and wrong. That was comfortable for him.

But it left no room for alternate views and opinions to be accepted. Because there could only be a "right" way and a "wrong" way in his world, he needed to protect his point of view fiercely. And, as my family and I knew all too well, being "wrong" was only reserved for those who were not him.

I wish I had the opportunity to tell him that all opinions could be purposeful in their own way. But then again, his response would have most certainly been: *"That's not reality! That's not the way the world works."*

As an insight, I was with my father when his soul decided to transition beyond this world. His physical body was in a coma, but his spirit spoke to me telepathically as I sat next to his hospital bed. He shared messages that were meant to be relayed to each family member, and then, with a voice that grew more distant as it rose beyond our earthly realm, he passionately expressed, *"You're right! It's so beautiful."*

My father had finally risen beyond his own limited belief system and could see the fullness of life without prejudice and resistance. He was now free to explore the infinite depths of his own miraculous being.

I'm so grateful that he shared that precious experience with me. It helped me to see the innocence of our spirits, beyond the confines of indoctrinated beliefs. We all want to know the freedom that comes with nonjudgment and individuality, but it's not easy to trust that path as valid and real if we've only known the contrast of "right" and "wrong" in the past.

Before that moment, I couldn't see that all the limitations my father was endeavoring to impose upon me were limitations that he had already accepted for himself. His efforts to be incessantly "right" were innocently birthed out of his indoctrinated fear of being "wrong."

If we resist our own perfectly imperfect natures by believing we must "measure up" to some high standard of righteousness, then we are denying the truths and responsibilities that are inherently ours to embrace.

Simply stated, we are essentially perfect in every way. But as soon as we limit that concept of perfection to some form of accepted norm or behavior, we deny all the parts of us that might exist outside that concept of accepted perfection.

And upon even deeper levels, if we are unwilling to accept every authentic part of ourselves, we may be redirecting responsibility for some of our personal truth.

Let's remember that we are the only ones who can be responsible for our own experiences. This includes our experiences of challenge, struggle, and pain too. There is never anyone else to either congratulate or blame for any of our very complicated life scenarios. They're all creations of our own making.

It's vital to begin accepting this truth because we can't authentically believe in our greatness if we have yet to accept responsibility for every single nuance of our personal journey.

This is where some hints of blame and shame might rise to the surface of your awareness. Be gentle with yourself if they do. We're going to heal these limited perceptions, together.

If you sense a bit of resistance to this teaching, I encourage you to compassionately breathe in a sacred way. Slowly inhale, while consciously envisioning that your breath is welcoming the purest of *healing light* directly into your heart space. From this point, the healing light expands into your entire body, both physically and energetically, blessing all.

Do this until you are again feeling relaxed and comfortable, remembering that every enlightened teaching is bringing new opportunities to heal the old and outdated beliefs that no longer serve.

> *"Nothing lies outside of your Self. When you begin to find peace in this knowing, life will begin to gracefully flow without struggle and resistance. Be still and know that it all lies within."*

> **~ Divine Spirit**

We can only affect change over that which is personal to our unique journey. So, we must establish a clearer understanding of all that is *personal* and all that is *impersonal*. Each time we confuse the two, we deny responsibility for that which is ours to shape and direct.

To illustrate this more clearly, I encourage you to imagine, just for a moment, that you have a clear understanding of what makes your world unique.

Imagine the fullness of all that is real to you. And now, allow yourself to push beyond the bounds of what feels personal to you. Are you able to sense some alternate truth or reality that exists "outwardly?"

If so, you've just connected to a thought or concept that lies beyond the bounds of your personal truth—and in doing so, you've just expanded the bounds of your personal truth.

If you have ever imagined sitting on some distant landscape, then that experience became real and personal to you as a conscious reality. Although it wasn't a physical experience, you believed in it, and you can now breathe life into it to deepen that connection, if you wish. However far removed it may be from your conscious focus and awareness each day—

that place now exists as an authentic part of your personal perception of reality.

Equally so, if you imagined a group of people who make this world a darker place, then that experience became real and personal to you as a conscious reality. Although those people aren't part of your immediate and discernible reality, you welcome that vibration of truth into "your world" by simply believing that they exist.

This is important because many beautiful souls who wish to create peace in their personal world still fill their mind with thoughts of injustice and cruelty that are happening in "the world" that exists outwardly. By doing this, they are creating an intimate relationship with that particular vibration of truth and are bringing it into their personal world. It is shaping their perception of reality because everything we interact with, in concept, becomes a part of our potential reality.

Whether we agree with something or we disagree with it, we accept it as real. Which means that the great big, expansive world that we sometimes feel so detached from is so much more intimate and relatable than we know.

The moment we interact with any thought, concept, or experience, it becomes personal to us.

> *"Life is in ever-flowing motion, touching all things. You are part of it all, in a grand existential way. But all Life can only be personal to you through 'experience.' All that you accept as truth, in each precious moment, shapes your reality. Therefore, that reality can only change when your concept of truth evolves and changes."*
>
> **~ Divine Spirit**

113

For many of us, the concept of free-will choice remains an enigma, even if we don't understand that it is. The simple truth is, we don't yet know what we don't know.

We think of "free-will choice" and apply it to the apparent choices in our life. Will we take a walk, or read a good book? Will we buy a new car, or visit an old friend? And, of course, these are all examples of free-will. But we have yet to recognize how deeply the concept of *free-will* impacts our basic foundational views of the world.

We accept certain conditions in life as deeply rooted structures that are inflexible and immutable. But all experience is a choice. It's all shaped by the way we see our potential reality.

If we believe that our financial abundance is limited, that we are responsible for the happiness of others, or that true love is hard to find, then we will accept these conditions as facts, not choices.

We don't yet recognize how malleable our world is and can be.

However, when we are ready to expand our understanding of what is possible, we will naturally attract new opportunities into our world, thereby creating greater choice for ourselves.

Since I was a young child, I have had repetitive dreams of battling darkness, manipulative forces, and mind-controlling factions. I learned early-on to accept them as a part of life since I never imagined that they could shift in any way. I considered them to be a principle part of my unique journey.

At the time, I was certain these dreams were teaching me to be strong so that I would be able to fight against every injustice that existed in the world, perceived and apparent. That was the level of consciousness I was able to comprehend.

What I didn't recognize at that time was that these dreams were also shaping the way I saw myself and all life. I became the brave warrior who could triumph through any hardship, simply because I believed that hardships were an inherent aspect of this human life.

No matter how intense the dreams became, I felt strong and capable. I never questioned whether I would overcome the unfathomable darkness that I faced in these dreams. Never, that is, until I started doubting my purpose and power in my earthly life.

In truth, I was beginning to feel incredibly unsafe in the physical world.

I was 32 years old by this point in time.

The person I most trusted to be my pillar of strength and support had recently abandoned me without notice or explanation. I know this is a story many of us are familiar with, but it caught me by surprise and shattered every sense of normalcy I had known.

This life-changing situation made me question all reality. It triggered a sense of vulnerability and hopelessness in me. For the first time in my life, I was processing a lot of irrational fears. And as a result of this, my dreams intensified.

They became more personal.

In each dream, I was no longer a witness to the greater injustice that might potentially be in the world. I was now the center of every tragic storyline. I was the one without power and choice.

I couldn't see through the illusion. So, I was beginning to believe, more and more fully, that my physical world was inherently challenging and unsupportive too. Everything felt restrictive and confining—and I didn't yet realize that it could be any other way.

The enlightened concept of *free-will choice* had not yet been introduced into my awareness.

A few years later, when I was eventually ready to expand my awareness, I naturally started to pay more attention to my dreams and to tap into greater details than I ever had. One of the first awe-inspiring details that became consistent throughout each dream was that I fought every fierce and immense foe with willpower alone.

I never used a weapon to defend myself. I only changed the outcome of every challenging scenario through confident mental focus and creative ingenuity. I was, essentially, using the power of my mind to defeat every defiant foe.

Actually, it was even more exciting than that! Each time I stood in my power, there was a radiant light that beamed from my hands, my heart, and my eyes. An indescribable force was moving through me to support me in any way that was needed.

This was the first time that I noticed this about myself.

Was this the way it had always been? Or was I fundamentally changing my reality to match my newly expanding consciousness? It was entirely possible that my innocent desire to "see clearly" was now presenting new choices and awareness for me to embrace, but I couldn't be sure. Everything was shifting so quickly.

I carried these new insights about myself back into my physical reality. I started to see myself facing every earthly challenge with the same confident willpower that I held in my dream state. I was focusing upon a supportive reality instead of a challenging one—and I was recognizing the impact that change could make.

My real-life experiences were shifting.

But now the dreams intensified, still, so that I might continue to see them in new ways. This time, I was in much closer proximity to each of the fierce (and sometimes monstrous) foes. I would prepare myself to defeat them in my usual way, and then begin to notice the presence of sadness and fear in their eyes.

They had all caused destruction in their path. But when I looked into their souls, I saw that it was never their intention to do so. Their motivations were always related to some form of self-preservation. They were really just wanting to be loved, and had become blind to the consequences of their aggressive actions and choices.

They needed compassion, not subjugation.

Again, I brought this new awareness back into my earthly existence. I shifted the way I looked at every challenging situation, trying to discern how I could be more compassionate in standing up for myself. I began to recognize that everything I perceived as a personal challenge was never intended to be so. There was always space to heal the situation, without "doing battle." Sometimes I changed the way I looked at a situation, and sometimes I changed the way I participated in it.

Regardless of my approach, the challenging scenarios were healing themselves.

It was not only my awareness that was transforming. My life was too! Because of all that I was learning in my dream state, I was systematically disempowering all the limiting assumptions that I had once believed to be constant and formidable.

As a result, new choices were continuously presenting themselves to me.

Still, the teaching wasn't yet complete. There was still one more awareness that needed to be understood before the dreams could predominantly come to an end.

I began to enter into the dreams after some devastating trauma had just taken place. In every individual dream, I searched for the manipulative force—the bringer of doom that had caused this massive disharmony. But they were nowhere to be found.

I could never find the source of the devastation.

So, in these dreams, I began directing my energy towards "saving" the souls that still felt wounded and imprisoned by their circumstances. I stood before each bright soul that had believed themselves to be a victim of the trauma, reminding them that they are safe and there is nothing to be fearful of.

But they didn't have the ability to understand my words. They were all entwined in the perceptions of victimhood, disempowerment, and lack. They had created a reality that reflected their perceptions of truth, and they weren't yet ready to move beyond it. It didn't matter if that reality existed in their mind-space only. It was real to them.

At the end of one of these dreams, I glanced upward. Amongst every soul that appeared to be lost and in illusion, were other souls just like me. Many of us were walking through the fields of strewn "survivors," reminding them that there was another reality waiting for them when they were ready.

With that understanding, I awoke from that dream. But it was not just the dream I awoke from; I also awoke from the illusion and the fantasy that had been accompanying me for countless years.

I finally realized that this life isn't laid out like an obstacle course that I must endure. Instead, it's an opportunity to face the countless challenges that I innocently create for myself.

And whether I see myself as the invincible warrior or the survivor that rises through all injustice, it makes no difference. *As long as I believe that the challenged path defines my reality, I will neglect to look deep within my own internal chasms for alternate perceptions of truth.*

This grand and eternal dream, called Life, is only as real as I believe it to be. As my awareness expands, so does my reality.

I had remained in my own limited perceptions for countless years because I didn't yet know that the choice was mine. But when my soul was ready to disempower the illusion, I found my way through.

I rarely have these dreams anymore because they were only with me as long as I needed them to be. Once I accepted the opportunity to "awaken," I could never see them in the same way I once did.

> *"Trust that as you wish to know your Self in greater ways, the paths you've known will grow and expand. For every journey, no matter the destination, leads you deeper into your Self."*
>
> ~ **Divine Spirit**

Our choices, made both consciously and subconsciously, shape our entire reality by directing energy with power and purpose. Whatever we place our focused attention upon becomes our reality.

When we are clear and confident in our choices, all life-force energy becomes focused upon those beliefs and energizes all that lies in support of them. And, as a fabulous little bonus to this practice of positive focus, all that is in opposition to that focused point will become disempowered and gracefully fall away.

Simply stated, if we remain focused upon peace, love, and joy, our focus is withdrawn from all that is in opposition to those energies. And if we are not actively energizing all that might be considered challenging and limiting, those energies will fall out of alignment with our personal perception of reality.

They will become impersonal concepts that exist in "the world" of infinite potential, but not "our world" of intimate experience.

In our soul's eternal journey, the presence of all chaos, conflict, and competition originally existed as mere potential in the full spectrum of possibilities that will always be. They were "implied" or "suggested" realities only—just as my father's perception of reality was implied to me. They only became personal to him and to me when we chose to intimately align with their energies at some point in time and space.

If we still perceive chaos, conflict, and competition in our current life experience, it can only be because we still empower those concepts to be real.

Each time we feed the sensations of fear and doubt, we validate the belief that there is something to fear and there is reason to doubt. Even anger and sorrow, as honorable as these emotions might be, actually empower the belief that there is injustice and pain in our personal world.

To clear the path forward into our *Divine Self*, we must compassionately ascend beyond the concepts of chaos and conflict. We must learn to see all free-will expression as purposeful, productive, and meaningful in relation to each soul's best and highest good.

If we no longer view any aspect of life as intrinsically opposing and intimidating, all varying expressions in life (regardless of how extreme) begin to harmonize and balance themselves within the whole.

It's absolutely possible for all to co-exist harmoniously without limiting anyone's creative expression.

However, I will admit that learning to harmoniously co-exist with *everything* and *everyone*, is sometimes a practice—one that we grow more confident in with each passing day.

There was a point when all appeared to be a bit chaotic and imposing in my life. I couldn't tune in to the quiet whisper of my own soul because the world around me had grown too loud.

I prayed for compassionate guidance.

In response to my soul's prayer for clarity and understanding, I was gifted with the sound of four words in my sleep. They repeated themselves throughout the night, holding energy and symbolism that was far greater than my awareness could initially comprehend.

I awoke with them still echoing through my mind, like a sacred mantra that never ends:

"A choir of cacophony."

"A choir of cacophony."

"A choir of cacophony."

121

In truth, I needed to look in the dictionary to learn whether the word "cacophony" was real. To my amazement, it was. It's what we sense when we're witness to a gaggle of two-year-olds all throwing tantrums simultaneously, or when we're in a crowded room where everyone is struggling to talk over each other.

Essentially, a "cacophony" is the sound of disorder and disharmony, while a "choir" is the sound of harmony and alignment.

How can there be *a choir of cacophony* if these two words, thoughts, and concepts lie in opposition to each other? How can anything sound "wonderful" and "disruptive" at the same time?

With these words, my spiritual guardians were introducing another sacred teaching to me, encouraging me to melt all sense of separation and disharmony.

Spirit was teaching me that Oneness is not equivalent to "sameness." Our human experience is meant to bring voice to all varieties of creative expression because individuality is what we are here for. It's only our *resistance to difference* that creates the discordance and conflict that we know.

By learning to honor each soul's precious choices as perfect and purposeful for their unique journey, we bring harmony to all that flows. There can be no conflict in a world that accepts all divine expressions as gracefully essential in their own ways.

All that is cacophonous becomes harmonious when we release from the belief that it "should be" any other way.

Our earthly perceptions of division and separation are all learned. They are only beliefs that we accept as true. But all beliefs have the ability to evolve and be reinterpreted at any time. They can only reflect our personal truths for as long as we empower them to.

I was walking in nature a few months ago, feeling exceedingly blessed for all that was unfolding in my life. As I stood in my power to offer sacred prayer to Source, a majestic Eagle called out to announce his presence. He was a powerful animal totem and spirit messenger for me. Coming from behind, he flew directly above my head, in exact alignment with my path forward.

He came to bless my prayer and show his loving support.

I was in gratitude and awe.

And then, just a minute or two after Eagle had appeared, an odd man (by my egoic assumption) walked towards me on the path, wearing no more than a polo-shirt tucked into his loosely fitting undies.

I was momentarily insulted, thinking that he could somehow desecrate my sacred experience—until a wave of pure, respectful laughter arose from within. With clarity and knowing, I suddenly realized that even he, too, was divine.

This brought me great comfort because I finally understood that "the world" could be as fanciful and dramatic as it wished to be, without ever distracting me from my own sacred path!

All things are part of the expansive and intricate whole, merging together into harmonious *symbiotic union*. Only my perceptions of separation, disorder, and disharmony could ever bring energy to those distracting experiences for me.

Because of that beautiful man and his unusual choice of attire, there was now a heightened measure of love in my heart.

All sense of separation is but a limited understanding of the greatest truth.

All can co-exist comfortably, without competition and conflict because all divine expression is perfect and precious in its own way. All serves its own sacred purpose.

And this is key.

Once we see all unique options as neutral alternatives within the full-spectrum of ever-flowing possibility, the conflict and separation that we sometimes place between all choices, realities, frequencies, and perceptions will naturally dissipate. A merging of all contrasting realities becomes possible.

As an example, we make significant effort to welcome peace and bliss into our lives through meditation, yoga practice, and joyful soul discovery, but then we also accept that this peace and bliss can be destroyed or diminished by the opposing energies we encounter in our physical reality.

We believe that a grumpy co-worker, a passive-aggressive loved one, or a drama-inclined neighbor can shake the positive focus we've cultivated for ourselves.

But, that's illusion.

They are only honoring their soul's path by expressing themselves freely. They are doing what is best for themselves, authentically, while offering us an opportunity to participate in their perception of reality—or not.

Too often, we believe that the choices of others are interfering with our empowered path. But that can never be true. We always have the right to remove ourselves, lovingly, from any experience that is less than inspiring. We do not have to explain ourselves or prove ourselves in these moments. *We only have to know ourselves*—so that we are confident in the choices we compassionately make for ourselves.

We are in a free-will experience, where all varying energies collectively exist. But we need never participate in any energy or experience that is less than comfortable and uplifting. It's always our privileged right to interact with only that which we choose.

CHAPTER ELEVEN

Our Masterful Self

"Freedom is a state of mind that cannot be taken from you. Only the belief that you are imprisoned, limited, or powerless can manifest that physical reality for yourself. And only the belief that you are free, empowered, sovereign, expansive, and all-knowing can create that physical reality for yourself too.

You are limited by nothing but your own belief."

~Divine Spirit

In vision state, I once found myself standing at the water's edge upon a large beach. An ever-flowing barrage of waves were knocking into me, one after the other, and it was a struggle to maintain my footing on the shifting sands. I didn't feel threatened or unjustly pushed by these waves. I simply felt that they were strong, and I needed to stand my ground in order to maintain my balance.

From above, a gentle presence reminded me that I could only feel uncertainty upon my path if, and when, I have forgotten who I am.

In that precise moment, as a reminder of my greater truth, a force of power surged through my whole body and spirit. I sensed the support of the sand and the earth, of the water and the wind, and of all that was beautiful and pure.

I felt invincible in this awareness, and knew that no wave could possibly shake my foundation when I stood proudly in remembrance of all I am.

This was a profound moment of awakening for my soul. At a deep state of authentic being, Spirit was reminding me that no outside force can ever shake my empowered *foundation* of truth. If I was feeling less than centered in my life, it was a sign that I had stepped into a submissive role in a victim-conscious reality, to some degree.

This vision reminded me that I was striving to do my best in a world that I had envisioned as unpredictable, unyielding, and impersonal.

I was only seeking to survive, not thrive.

In order to reclaim my personal power, I needed to remember that all universal source flows through me and supports me upon my journey. I am the master of my experience, in all ways.

The waves were only there because it's their nature to flow. They have never held any power over me, beyond that which I was willing to give them. I am, and have always been, the director of limitless resource within my Self, no matter what appears outwardly—*and so are you.*

I think, if we're honest with ourselves, that we all resonate with a sense of disempowerment at times.

I think we all move through the genuine cycles of belief and disbelief. It's a natural part of our soul's evolutionary journey. But we can learn to move through these moments of doubt and insecurity with greater confidence and ease—if we take a moment to remember the immensity of all we truly are.

As the masterful creator of our own reality, all universal energy reacts and responds to our personal energy.

Our shifting thoughts and beliefs always have the ability to directly impact our immediate experience because at a deep and profound state of authentic being, we are the director, designer, and sovereign master of all we see.

This precious truth is immutable and does not change according to any shifting "tide" or circumstance. It doesn't precisely mandate what we must experience upon our journey into free expression; it only states that whatever we choose for our Self, will effortlessly manifest as our reality.

We have known pain in the past because we have believed that pain was a construct of our human reality. We have also believed that challenge and suffering were inherent elements of this existence. And so, a path of "survival" became our only way through.

Now, however, we are being offered an opportunity to imagine a joyful existence of infinite wonder, beyond the concepts of survival and challenge. We are being reminded that pain is just as much a choice as peace is.

Are you ready to re-evaluate your entire understanding of what is real and true?

In order to become the master creator of our own destiny, we must begin to take responsibility for all that is a part of our precious life. If we see ourselves as trapped and limited in any capacity, we will be perpetuating that belief. But if we begin to envision ourselves as free and empowered, we will be seeding that reality as a viable path upon our journey.

The more energy we place into any accepted belief, the more it becomes our manifest reality. This happens because our thoughts are *constant directives* to all universal source.

If I believe that my life is a challenge, I will attract a parade of ever-flowing challenges. Each time a new challenge appears, I will believe that the challenge is validating my belief. But, in actuality, my belief is creating that challenge.

This awareness can be life-changing for all who are ready to welcome progressive change into their lives.

If we continue to blame a flat tire, a thunderstorm, or an old friend for our misfortunes, we will only perpetuate the belief that we are vulnerable to some outside force. That belief will strengthen within our fundamental core, which defines our personal understanding of what is true and real, and we will attract greater "misfortune."

Thankfully, the opposite is also true.

If we begin to remember that we are always blessed and loved, regardless of all that appears, we begin to look for the blessing, the solution, and the positive outcome in all moments. Our energy, thoughts, and beliefs will be focused upon finding the beauty that may be, so we will attract and align with all of the beauty that can be.

The presence of a flat tire, a thunderstorm, or a miscommunication with an old friend can remain the same in each scenario; but the outcome will vary according to the *thoughts* and *beliefs* that represent our fundamental truth in that moment.

Knowing "blessing" upon our journey has no greater intrinsic value than knowing "challenge." The outcome is never pre-ordained by karma, luck, fate, or divine intervention. It's always a factual response to the thoughts and beliefs we align with at subtle levels of authentic being.

Are you ready to see yourself as the *empowered force* behind your shifting world of circumstance?

Your thoughts, actions, and choices will always be the controlling factor in your malleable reality. Never are you without influence upon your environment or your experience! *By natural order and decree, you are always responsible for your own energy.*

To demonstrate this truth further, I'd like to share a profound "mystery teaching" with you. (I consider a mystery teaching to be any lesson which comes directly from Source so that we might easily understand the mysteries of this universe and all reality more fully.)

This particular mystery teaching brings deeper understanding to the sacred Buddhist mantra, *"Om Mani Padme Hum."* It's a reminder that all life is greater than it appears. We can choose to focus upon that which is evident and plain, or upon that which exists at a deeper level of authentic being.

Early in my journey, I was passionately drawn to this mantra without any logical understanding of its meaning. I knew that *"Behold, the jewel within the lotus!"* was its most popular translation, but those words confounded me. I couldn't break away from the structured meaning they represented.

Then, one night, I began to experience another series of profound dream visions that would re-structure how I connected to the sound, the wisdom, and the power that these syllables convey.

In the most impactful dream, I was in deep survival mode. I was being chased by various souls, all of whom wished to destroy me. Whether by sword, fist, or machine gun, I was being aggressively attacked. I kept searching for someone to bring peace to the injustice, but no one in the survival-based community could understand what I was complaining about.

I felt utterly alone in this battle. My only choice was to keep fighting or to give up.

Then, suddenly, I came across a group in an open temple environment. All were chanting this sacred mantra, *"Om Mani Padme Hum,"* but I did not hear those words at first. I only heard empty sounds being repeated in drone-like fashion.

All who were present seemed to be responding to the direction of one authority figure at the front of the space. I frantically rushed to the side of that teacher, in hopes that he would listen to me. But as I drew nearer to him, I was unexpectedly touched by his enormity of presence. He appeared to be much greater, bolder, and wiser than seemed possible for any "mere human" to be.

I still made great efforts to explain the danger I was in, but his energy was unexpectedly soothing my desire to speak. While holding on to the connection he held with each student in that space, he turned to me and telepathically encouraged me to silence my thoughts. Without any verbal communication, he inspired me to lay down all resistance so that I might open to a greater truth.

My body instinctively laid back into Savasana—a yogic pose of total surrender—and I trusted the experience to guide me.

This wise teacher silently removed a necklace from his neck and placed it around my own. Intuitively, this gesture told me that I was no longer lost. I was home, safe and accepted. I belonged. I was loved.

Then his finger moved forward (in slow-motion, Yoda style) and gently opened several portals of energy all over my body. With each point of activation, waves of energy flooded through, and the sound of *"Om Mani Padme Hum"* began to rise from within.

As if they were pure expressions of my heart's beat, the primal sounds began to awaken my soul.

I physically awoke from that dream with a new and enlightened understanding of what *"Behold, the jewel within the lotus!"* represents.

At the beginning of the dream, I was reacting to my environment. I was viewing my own safety, security, and identity according to that which appeared outwardly. I was participating in a version of reality that embraced survival as a commonplace experience. In that mental space, the only thoughts which had filled my awareness were in response to that which existed outwardly.

By the end of the dream, however, my awareness had shifted. I was no longer resonating with a survival mentality. *I was blissfully connected to the universe within my soul.*

My focus had gracefully shifted to a point within.

In that moment of union between myself and universal consciousness, I felt connected to all realms of truth, seen and unseen. Without a single word to tell me what was flowing through, I understood.

That which is pure and true cannot be explained.

It must be felt.

It flows through all things, all life, and all moments, but can only be intimately known at the level of comprehension that we are able to comfortably embrace.

The indefinable essence which lies within all life-form, in all universal expansiveness, is the "jewel". It's what brings all to a state of oneness and connectedness. It's what directs all, shapes all, and empowers all.

It is, in fact, what I was sensing as being "greater than mere human" when I first approached this teacher. That which appears outwardly is only a distraction from the greatest truth; *it's the vehicle through which all universal consciousness expresses itself.*

It's actually our physical essence—as the lotus or as our body—which allows all universal consciousness to discover itself from outside of itself.

This teacher was able to radiate pure wisdom and light to me while in his physical form because he had been cultivating a deep connection with the *infinite spirit* that lies within. He already understood himself to be more than that which appeared. He understood himself to be all things, seen and unseen.

In my own ecstatic reunion with Source during this dream vision, I could sense that I was that immense force of infinite life-expression—*and it was me.* That which I had so longed to connect to and find was within me all along. It was my own innocent heartbeat and untethered spirit.

From the clouded perceptions of fear and survival, at the beginning of this dream vision, my own internal voice of love and truth was overpowered. My attention was placed outwardly, waiting for solutions and support to be presented from somewhere outside myself.

I was participating in, and therefore empowering, that paradigm of reality. *The challenges were real because I believed them to be real.*

By accepting our infinite nature with power and purpose, we can recognize that we are always the center of our universe. We are always intimately connected to all expansive potential. No separation between our Self and all universal consciousness can ever be.

"When we speak of divine remembrance, it's not that we speak of returning to the essence, identity, or form of what was. It's the remembrance of being FREE and INFINITE that we wish to awaken. We speak of formless empowerment in ever-creative motion. For you are the cosmic dancer on the sea of timeless existence. There is no-thing that you are not."

~ Divine Spirit

And even when we accept that we are the cosmic dancer on the sea of timeless existence, it is still quite possible to become a bit lost in the "how" of it all. As long as we identify with our physical bodies and minds as our understanding of Self, we will always find it difficult to identify with a grander understanding of Self.

In order to see ourselves as infinite in any way, we have to stretch our awareness to become the "jewel" within the body and the mind. We are the life-force that empowers all that is physical. Without this cosmic force of indefinable energy within, our bodies would become lifeless and our minds would become powerless.

Our physical experience is sustained by the divine consciousness that touches, awakens, and energizes all things.

This truth is constant and immutable.

Without the Light within, we cease to exist.

This knowing allows us to compassionately conclude that we are not our body or our mind. We are universal source, embodied, for a sensory-rich experience.

"The light you seek is not with you, as a companion upon your fateful journey. It is you, full and complete. You are the breath of life and the dawn of all creation! You are as infinite and expansive as you allow yourself to be."

~ Divine Spirit

I believe this completely. And still, I find it difficult to integrate this greater fundamental truth into my current understanding of Self. After lifetimes of believing that I am bound to the limitations of my physical body, it's taking me a long moment to shift my awareness and fully accept that I am the Light of all universal source.

I can, however, confidently accept that there are infinite aspects of my *Divine Self* that I have yet to recognize and acknowledge. With this understanding, I can allow my awareness to gently expand, without contradicting or denying the parts of me that still feel quite sensitive and uncertain upon higher planes of consciousness.

As I grow more comfortable in a multi-dimensional view of my Self—one that allows me to simultaneously co-exist at more than one level of conscious awareness—I see that I am not bound to only that which currently appears evident. I can shift my awareness to carefully tune in to the wise master that I already am, upon higher planes of consciousness, if I so wish.

"You see your Self as existing in all that feels so intimate and personal to you now. But do not doubt the magnificence that you are. You also exist upon higher realms of consciousness! You are so much more than you imagine your Self to be."

~ Divine Spirit

135

The more we rise in awareness, unity, and love, the more we feel intimately connected to the wisest aspects of our Self that are eternally guiding and supporting our journey. The belief that any influence outside of our own infinite nature has the power to impose its will upon our experience, or wield control over our dominion of Light, is illusion. It's false perception and holds no truth from a divine state of being.

There is no condition or circumstance that can ever hold us back from respectfully exploring all that we are capable of. This includes the people we know, the environments we are in, and the foundations we are part of. *The power to positively affect change in our life is always ours.*

Once we are no longer willing to surrender to less than we are worthy of, we will recognize this. We will find a rising strength within. And that pristine force of formidable determination will instinctually align us with the energies, frequencies, and elements we wish to know and embrace.

Simply said, when our will to succeed, achieve, and thrive becomes greater than the doubts and fears that keep us tethered to a surrendered state of subjugation, we will find our empowered way through. One step at a time, we will clear the path that lies before us.

There is, however, one point of importance that I must be quite clear about. We can only participate in the energies, frequencies, and experiences that we feel entirely worthy of. We can't even begin to direct ever-expanding abundance and prosperity into our life until we feel genuinely worthy of it.

So, we must create space for all deeply hidden insecurities to be compassionately healed, or they will continue to naturally undermine our soul's growth. They will create a subliminal resistance to all the beauty and bounty we are making great efforts to invoke.

It's vital at this stage of awareness to confidently believe that we are extraordinary and wondrous, as an uncompromising truth.

Even in our perceived imperfection, we must trust that we are authentically precious and worthy. There can be no perpetuating opposition to our chosen path and inspired journey.

I recall a time when I had once gathered with a beautiful group of truth seekers in a sacred circle. We had merged our heart intentions and welcomed a message from the higher realms.

A collective of brilliant guides and guardians appeared to surround our circle in love, and one came forward to speak for the whole. I recognized his bright essence as Lord Melchizedek, ascended master and teacher of Light. Radiant, wise, and full of grace, his energy touched us all, while sweetly echoing these words into our heart-space:

> *"It is time, Dear Ones, to appreciate the generosity of your own precious heart. You give so much, to so many, without giving value to all that you most magnificently are. We see you and all that you are abundantly worthy of. We wish to bless you now, showering you with all that inspires your soul. But we can only gift you with that which you are genuinely ready to welcome and receive. Be clear in your intentions and desires. If you hold doubt or resistance at any level, you will naturally deny the fullness of all that is already yours. See yourselves as worthy. See yourselves through the eyes of love."*

Two vital truths become clear with this message.

The first truth reminds us that in order to create a world of bliss, love, joy and peace for ourselves, we must believe that we are fully worthy of these experiences. If we continue to see ourselves through the eyes of doubt, imperfection, and shame, we'll naturally resist all blessings at an unseen level of being.

The second truth reminds us that we never journey alone. Every step is continuously supported by countless planes of existence. Whether we recognize it or not, we are always co-creating with universal source in infinite measure. Our thoughts and prayers are valued by all heavenly realms, and only a whisper from our truest heart-space will bring the blessings we seek.

Even our concept of "humility" has no place upon this path of empowered understanding because all universal source honors and supports us. *We are not earning the right to be blessed.* We are accepting the blessings that are already ours to embrace and behold.

This truth cannot be doubted, because the mere thought of unworthiness will actually bind us to an experience of unworthiness, for as long as we believe it to be true.

> *"Each infinite plane of existence is always available to you upon your journey. When all is comfortable and aligned, your spirit will joyfully discover all that powerfully awaits. There is no boundary holding you clear from discovering these infinite aspects of your Self. When you are ready to see, to feel, and to be—without resistance—all veils will lift, allowing you to move through all dimensions of infinite being with ease and grace."*

> ~ **Divine Spirit**

CHAPTER TWELVE

All That Is Divine

*"You are the designer of your reality and
you are the beauty of all you design! You
are divine source expressing yourself,
freely. Blast through the state of human
consciousness that teaches you to be
insignificant, inferior, or imperfect in any
way. Embrace the knowing that you are
divine consciousness manifest in human
ecstasy."*

~ **Divine Spirit**

As a compassionate insight, I must point out that some of the
religious practices that we've trusted in the past, center their
focus around the perception that we are inherently flawed
and sinful. They encourage us to believe that divine grace is
something that we must earn and then strive to keep, as if it
can be granted and then rescinded.

After many years and lifetimes of indoctrination according to
these values, it is quite possible (if not probable) that we
strongly believe in our limited self-worth. Much healing still
needs to take place for those of us who have reverently
accepted these false truths as "divine" proclamation.

Thankfully, the healing begins now, by gently accepting that
we are inherently worthy and can be no less.

For those of us still struggling with the concept of being worthy, it will help us to remember that true divinity is not a state of elusive grandeur and authority. It cannot be found in an exclusive dominion of attainment reserved for a chosen few. And it cannot be bound to any definable point or attribute.

Divinity is the boundless expression of all that is love.

It's who we are—and yet so much more than we imagine ourselves to be.

We complicate our perceptions of *God* and *Divinity* by attaching countless assumptions to our understanding. But, it's truly simple. They are one and the same essence, found in all things and all moments of time and space. There is no place that God is not and there is no place that Divinity is not.

They are both all-inclusive states of consciousness and can be no less. Any limited or fear-based values that we have attached to these boundless concepts are but assumed understandings of their greatest truth.

God is love and Divinity is the perfect embodiment of that love (beyond all perception of lack, limitation, and separation).

Or vice-versa. It's all the same.

We can also recognize God and Divinity as Spirit, Source, the One, the All, Creator, and Creation. All contrast and separation are but an illusion at this level of infinite awareness. The name we give it does not matter. It is always the singular force, spirit, and essence that breathes Life into all things, but controls nothing.

It is the totality of all that is, seen and unseen. Which also implies that you and I are intricate aspects of the One, and all that is Divine. *It's our greatest state of personal, intimate, and authentic being.*

From this state of elevated truth, all voices are united into wholeness. Individuality does not exist, and all perceptions of being separate are baseless and untenable.

There is nothing to bow down to and nothing to praise as more worthy than ourselves because there is only love flowing endlessly into our heart-space, wishing to remind us of who we truly are.

This is what I innocently connected to in those first prayers for answers and understanding, so many years ago.

I called out to God, from my limited understanding of who God was, but it was my own *Divine Self* that continuously spoke to me, as God, as Blessed Mother, as Buddha, and more.

> *"When you are ready to see, clearly, all veils will gracefully lift to unite you with the boundless wonder of all you are. For in truth, there is no-thing that you are not."*
>
> **~ Divine Spirit**

In this extraordinary journey of self-discovery, we sometimes move bravely into realms of understanding that challenge our confident perceptions of truth and reality. We are asked to slowly stretch our awareness beyond all that once brought us comfort, so that we might accept an expansive reality that cannot always be validated by logic alone.

Are you ready for this? Are you willing to strip yourself bare of every pre-conceived notion so that you might dance in the infinite realms of your own sacred consciousness?

When we begin to trust our own instincts as true and authentic, we never need to trust the subjective truth of another in order to understand ourselves. We will have direct connection to our own source of "verifiable" truth; *a truth that is confirmed by our own intuitive knowing.*

I initiated my very first prayer from a deep space of fear, sorrow, and desperation. But when compassion and love was shared with me, from a divine state of being, I trusted it as real and true. I accepted the blessings as authentic, even though they were in direct opposition to so many of the beliefs I had held up until that time.

My trust in that first loving interaction led to a second inspired experience, and a third, and so on. I was re-evaluating all that I had previously accepted as true because I was finally ready to trust my Self.

Even though I couldn't yet understand why I was willing to trust these intuitive insights, it was natural for me to do so. As long as I stayed centered in what felt comfortable for me, personally, I was able to trust my own direct insights over the implied truths that had been taught to me by so many others throughout time.

An unprecedented sense of strength, paired with a whole lot of unbridled curiosity, was awakening within me. I was willing to bravely disempower all perceptions of self-doubt, judgment, blame, fear, and unworthiness because they no longer felt like the only options in my world.

I was beginning to sense a world that was so much greater and more supportive than I had previously recognized. Deep within, I knew it was time for all sense of judgment and false expectation to compassionately heal itself, so that a greater understanding of authentic truth could begin to guide my path forward.

Like me, perhaps you have been holding yourself accountable to unnatural measures and expectations of perfection, too. Many of us have innocently established interpretations and ideals for all that would define us as "perfect" and "worthy," without ever recognizing that we were doing so.

We have been stacking these "ideals" up in our psyches for as long as we can remember. So, we can barely recognize that by seeing ourselves in contrast to these arbitrary "ideals," we are placing great attention upon our inadequacies, our shortcomings, and our flaws.

At this level of limited consciousness, we will only accept ourselves as "worthy" when we have proven our worth by some standard of arbitrary measurement. But once we attain one standard of measurement, we will impose another upon ourselves—and we will continue to do so time after time.

If we were able to find some measure of validation and approval outwardly the first time, we will continue that pattern of behavior as if it were a proven course of action.

This is why we can sometimes see ourselves as better than or less than another soul. We believe that one of us has reached some goal or expectation that the other has yet to attain. And although that original method of standardized value was arbitrarily set, it has come to represent a form of acceptable measurement for us.

Without truly understanding our motivations, we have learned to see our personal value and worth in comparison to another—*instead of focusing on the unique beauty we each represent.*

We can continue to acknowledge this practice of contrast and comparison in regard to the other souls around us, or we can expand our vision to include our perceived relationship between ourselves and all that is "divine."

It's quite possible that we see ourselves as less than pure, perfect, and wondrous in comparison to all that exists beyond our current perceptions of awareness. As long as I personally regarded Divinity (with a big "D") as greater than my Self and all humanity, I could never fully open to the greatness that "I am."

I had to move through a process of stripping away the illusion of "superior greatness" from my concept of Divinity—so that it could become the simple truth of all we are. When it no longer existed outside of my Self, I was able to acknowledge that pure vibration of all-encompassing truth as precious divinity (with a little "d") and no more.

In its purest form, *divinity* is the whole essence of boundless "being."

Being free. Being authentic. Being real. Being all. Being nothing. Being you. Being me.

It's the gift of being—without bounds, conditions, or limitations.

Imagine that you are being offered an opportunity to be everything you could imagine yourself to be. And you never have to place any attention on what you "should" or "should not" be.

There is no box to stand in.

There is nothing to hold you back from being free.

We are speaking of a pure state of consciousness, where all is aligned and in harmony within itself. It requires no pretense of subjugation from another (as is often implied by many of our major religions) for it to be all that it naturally is. In other words, there is no need to bow down or diminish your Self in order to prove your love or your worth.

Our perceptions of a great divine source—separate from and more wondrous than ourselves—are all falsely assumed. They were originally inspired by myths, told by those who were doubting their own precious divinity.

Spirit tells me a story of when we all lived in graceful harmony, long before this cycle of recorded history. Those who were embodied in Light were present in our earthly experience, serving as great beacons of illumination, strength, and wisdom for those who were exploring a human reality.

There was no sense of "comparison" between the two forms of being (those who were earthly and those who transcended earthly form) because each knew that they were a reflection of the other's greater Light. Illusion, to its fullest capacity, was only an available concept, not an embraced reality.

At some point, as the journey of soul exploration took some souls deep into the shadows of doubt and fear, the perception that those who were embodied in Light were separate from those who were embodied in physical form, took shape. Distance was created between all that was divine (connected and in harmony) and all that was searching (in doubt and insecurity).

To honor the free-will of those who did not wish to journey with those who were embodied in Light, a veil of separation was created. Those who were brothers and sisters in Light— *truly a part of our soul family*—removed themselves to be present beyond the veil.

They did not abandon those who wished to journey with them. *They only removed their presence from the physical planes!*

From that moment on, only those who trusted their hearts to reveal the greatest truth could sense their presence. Only those who knew the purity of all-encompassing love within themselves could lift the veils of separation and bridge the gap between all that is earthly and all that is divine.

We can say that we are the descendants of those ancient beings, but truly, *we are those ancient beings reincarnate.*

We might have been the ones who acted in fear or the ones who remained connected throughout. It matters not. We are being offered an opportunity to see beyond the veil, once again, to trust these divine beings as part of our intimate family in Light. In doing so, from our earthly form, we begin to undo the lifetimes of generational trauma that were originally placed in motion at that time.

It is time to lift the veils of separation by remembering that we are all one—and can be no less.

Buddha, a great master of truth and compassion, assisted me in breaking through my own assumed perceptions of limited self-worth, in comparison to all that was divine. He presented himself to me as a loving brother and patiently worked with me until I saw my Self as I saw him. It was a supreme test of my self-worth, and it forever changed the way I see each of us, authentically.

But before I tell this story, let me say that I had been raised to humble myself before all forms of assumed authority.

If another soul was older than myself, had accomplished something magnificent, wore a uniform of any imaginable color, or held a title of self-proclaimed awesomeness, I was encouraged to honor them blindly. At least, this is the message that I inferred from societal standards and guidelines. I was rarely encouraged to look into someone's eyes to discern their integrity and truth.

I will not say that I actually followed through with that form of flattery and blind submissiveness, but it's the expectation that was imparted upon me. It caused me to continuously create distance between myself and my community, because I naturally shielded myself from those who felt like a false-authority figure, and I humbled myself to those who were authentic in their essence and truth.

In other words, if someone was an impostor to the authority they claimed, I disconnected from them emotionally. And if they were the real deal, I felt unworthy.

Although I had people around me at every stage of life, I felt intimately connected to very few.

My brother, Buddha, came to me very early upon my journey into remembrance. He came at a time when shadowed thoughts still filled my mind, and I could easily see myself through the eyes of pain, struggle, and judgment.

I had known genuine moments of sweet bliss in my spiritual practice, but I still spent most of my time in fear and distrust. Buddha appeared as a spiritual mentor, to still my mind and expand my perception of Self.

His presence especially triggered my limited sense of self-worth because, prior to that moment, I had very little knowledge and awareness of who Buddha was. It was comfortable for me to receive messages from God, Blessed Mother, and Archangel Michael because they were within my personal belief system. But who was I to imagine that Buddha, the enlightened one, wished to speak to *me*?

I couldn't understand why Buddha would present himself to me when I held no discernable reverence (beyond one of great respect) for him. I felt like a stranger who was unworthy of his blessings.

But that is how he progressively changed my whole view of life, in every beautiful way.

If I resisted his presence, to align with my feelings of unworthiness, he looked deep into my eyes and filled me with waves of eternal love. I say "eternal" because in that flow of divine love, all time was united and present. There was no sense of separation between my Self and his bright essence. It felt as if we had journeyed through the cosmos as one heart and were now blessed enough to find each other again, in this momentary space.

In those moments of heart connection, Buddha stood before me, gazing deeply into my eyes, telepathically communicating repeatedly:

"*I Am You and You Are Me.*"

Each time those words reverberated through me, I felt Buddha's energy merge into mine and my energy merge into his, creating a brilliant infinity symbol of energy and light between us.

I acknowledged his words as a conceptual truth and felt my sense of Self expand in his energetic embrace. However, my beautiful brother, Buddha, had wished for me to repeat these words back to him, in power and truth.

I could not do this. I could not even *feign* to do this.

In my logical mind, at that time, it was a sacrilege to even imagine that I was equal to Buddha in any way.

But he did not give up on me. For several months, without a single word of judgment, he continued to repeat this practice of gazing deeply into my eyes with only love flowing through, telepathically communicating "*I Am You and You Are Me.*"

I can no longer recall how many times we danced like this, but I do remember that my response to this pure gift of love and acceptance began to slowly shift.

At first, I could not imagine repeating these words back to him, for fear of being pretentious and committing a sin (a belief that still remained from my childhood indoctrination). But slowly, my resistance began to melt. At first, I was able to imagine repeating those words in my mind. Then, I was able to imagine whispering them out loud. Bit by bit, my comfort grew, until one day, I was able to stand confident and proud.

On that particular day, when nothing appeared different from any other day, my beautiful brother, Buddha, and I moved through the familiar motions of gazing deeply into each other's eyes so that I might once again be offered an opportunity to passionately express, *"I Am You and You Are Me."*

In that perfect moment, my body became a tuning fork for waves of indescribable energy. I allowed my words to reverberate through all expanse of time and space, as I boldly expressed:

"I Am You and You Are Me!"

In direct response to my proud declaration, Buddha's energy expanded outwardly, until it had filled the entire horizon and all I could see before me. He wanted to remind me that I am *that* expansive and phenomenal too.

I finally understood! This whole teaching was to open a gate of awe-inspiring truth within me.

Buddha's voice began to powerfully echo these words into my own expansive being:

> *"And now you see, that in order for you to do all that you have come here to do, you must believe that you are THE most radiant, powerful, perfect, and pure being that can be. And still, you must remember that you are no greater than any other being."*

That was it. The teaching was now complete.

How could I begin to imagine my greatest potential and truth if I continued to remain inside the box of insignificance and unworthiness?

Through this teaching, Buddha was not trying to tell me that he and I were the same person. He was showing me, with great compassion and grace, that all the earthly and unearthly potential that flows through his great spirit also flows through my own.

We are both unique expressions of the same brilliant light. We have both been birthed from the pure heart of divine consciousness.

From this perspective of truth, we are one.

With this realization, I understood that all previous beliefs of imperfection, insignificance, and inferiority were founded in illusion and fear. They can never hold any truth or purpose upon the highest planes of divine consciousness. It was time to begin seeing myself through the eyes of love and acceptance, so that I might clear all false perceptions and accept the beauty that I most genuinely am.

I was ready to see clearly.

But first, I had to stretch my awareness to reinterpret what "love" truly represented, without clinging to the prejudices that I had been taught.

Love isn't something that can be earned with good behavior or secured with passionate vows. It is an all-encompassing state of acceptance and appreciation that allows us to honor all forms of life-expression as perfect and purposeful.

It can never be confined to any altered or elevated state of awareness because it's always available to us, in all moments, regardless of circumstance.

Love is the undeniable force we often sense when we are in deep meditation and heart-centered prayer. It holds no attachments, tethers, or weights. It's freely offered, freely given, and freely shared.

In fact, any expression of love that offers less than this pure state of ecstatic being, is only an amateur's attempt to know love.

> *"From every divine plane of authentic being, only love flows to you, in infinite measure. Any less is but a construct of your free-will and imagination."*
>
> ~ **Divine Spirit**

Love is what we most yearn for because it's our most comfortable connection to all that is divine. Our souls know this. *We, as divine beings, are birthed from love, in love, for the express purpose of being love, incarnate.*

We may feel as though we are lost in a fog of confusion and disbelief for a moment, but our ultimate truth is constant and immutable. Beneath all the pain, disappointment, shame, and fear, we wish to know love, fully and completely.

In the purest states of divine love there is no need to defend, protect, hide, or isolate any aspect of our Self in order to know its light. The perception that we are imperfect or unworthy is a learned assumption. It's an indoctrinated falsehood that is naturally rising to higher planes of consciousness at this time.

As an interesting observation, I strongly believe this explains why so many are choosing paths of direct connection to God and Source. We are no longer comfortable with the limited promises and vows of a strictly religious path. We are ready to be loved and respected instead of intimidated and belittled. But that is definitely a topic for another book, at another time.

We have all been birthed in love (regardless of the physical circumstances) and our lives are sustained in love (from the highest realms of divine truth). All energies that remain in opposition to this pure vibration of love are continuously being reprogrammed, or at least re-evaluated, daily.

As we rise into greater curiosity of our own divine nature, all veils of separation gracefully fade away and uncensored illumination begins to light the way ahead.

This is the epic journey of awakening our *Divine Self*.

CHAPTER THIRTEEN

Discernment and Truth

"As a being of heightened awareness, you are beginning to see the beauty in the shadow, the divinity in the pain, and the perfection in the illusion. Sometimes it's only through these life experiences that your soul can find the vital clarity, healing, and strength that it most desires."

~ Divine Spirit

If all things are divine and created in love, we must accept that even shadows, fear, pain, and loss come from the same sacred source that joy, pleasure, and peace do. Beneath every authentic perception of limitation, there is an understanding that all experiences essentially bring us deeper into our own soul's growth and evolution.

Every shadow is present because it yearns to be touched by the light. It craves to come back into wholeness by remembering that it's more than just a shadow.

Life unfolds in unexpected ways. Often, it's to provide us with valuable opportunities to bring balance and harmony to the shadowed perceptions we already hold within.

However, let me be very clear. Knowing "shadow" (as any variation of limitation or lack) does not make us "shadowed."

153

We are pristine beings of Light, exploring the shadows through experience only. We do this so that we might see ourselves through a new lens of awareness.

These experiences never need to define our journey or negate the magnificence of all we are. Through every shadowed experience that may be, we remain connected to the boundless Light that is.

Buddha explained it to me this way:

> *"As you awaken to your divine nature, life will continue to present itself in creative ways, but challenges and conflict will no longer define your reality because you will no longer feel limited by the circumstances of any individual moment. The world has not changed. Only you have changed! And that changes everything."*

These words carried me through a lot of the challenges that did, in fact, continue to present themselves in my life. They brought me the very precious gift of discernment. They taught me that the appearance of challenge and chaos didn't actually mean that challenge and chaos were part of my personal reality.

In order to fully assimilate this teaching into my awareness, I was learning how to transform each stress-inducing scenario into a reminder that I was blessed, supported, and loved. And that's no tiny enterprise to undertake. It takes focus and fortitude to stay centered in your own empowered perceptions of truth while the self-defeating ones are still present and trying to prove how real they are.

This is why we need to practice personal discernment in our lives. If we focus upon our own truth in the midst of all contrasting truths, we will always be able to find peace in the middle of any situation that might be.

But how do we know which truth to trust?

How do we know which truth will most benefit us and our soul's evolutionary growth? It's not easy to see clearly when we are already feeling overwhelmed and confused. Under these circumstances, it's even quite natural to make decisions based in fear without even noticing that we are motivated in this way.

Because we are not always comfortable in the darkest places of life, both within ourselves and within the world around us, we have learned to fear the shadows of all that is uncertain and unknown. And, because we are not comfortable in admitting our vulnerability, we create stories to disguise that fear or to deny that insecurity.

Essentially, we have all created belief systems to either keep ourselves separate from the shadows of life, or to make grand excuses for the shadows of life.

We have not yet been taught to understand the delicate relationship that exists between the shadow and the light, both within ourselves and within the world around us. But understanding this relationship is one of the greatest keys to awakening our *Divine Self*.

Acceptance of all inherent truth brings clarity, discernment, empowerment, freedom, and peace.

It is time to fully remember who we are.

I have always enjoyed my solitude in this life. I am not someone who is motivated by the promises of great success or accomplishment, and too much attention has always made me feel a bit vulnerable. But these natural tendencies, to live quietly, were holding me back from living life fully. So, a few years ago, I began to focus upon healing the parts of me that were comfortable in hiding and remaining unseen.

In response to my soul's prayers, I had a phenomenal healing experience with Mary Magdalene, in vision state. Up until that point, I had never felt Mary Magdalene's presence with me, personally. This was a new experience for me.

She came to bring a deep lesson of love and forgiveness—one that would continue to expand from that day forward.

I happened to be in a completely relaxed state when she first appeared. To be accurate, I was in the middle of receiving a massage, and had not intended to have any deeper spiritual experience at that time. But that is often how our guardians in the spirit realm make a deeper connection. They come through when we are most open to receive, without expectation or attachment.

While surrendered, I suddenly sensed Mary Magdalene standing before me. I instantly knew her to be Mary Magdalene, without doubt. It felt as though we had walked through all time together, and it was perfectly natural to reunite in this moment.

While her eyes sparkled with the purest of loving emanations, she held out her hand to me and powerfully, yet compassionately, said *"It's time to come home."*

My spirit jumped in excitement, as I had first considered that she was welcoming my soul home to France. (Coincidentally, I had just purchased plane tickets to visit France and I was already aware of Mary Magdalene's connection to that sacred land.) But then, my attention was drawn to the right, where I recognized an ancient aspect of myself kneeling down in the shadows.

This was the part of me she was speaking to.

156

This ancient part of me, that lived within my Self at hidden depths, was heartbroken over all the countless times that I had represented less than light upon this earth. I still felt her pain as if it were my own. Eons of sorrow, shame, and guilt were debilitating her ability to see clearly. And, by extension, these deeply seeded emotions were still debilitating my own ability to see clearly too.

This ancient part of me had never been healed. She was still guiding my subtle perceptions of reality, making it difficult for me to see beyond the torment I had once known.

Through the empathic connection that I held with this ancient part of me, I could sense that I had known great darkness in my lives. In fact, I had embodied the darkest of the dark, the cruelest of the cruel, and the most treacherous of the treacherous.

As I trusted this to be true, my heart began to shatter and break all over again. How could this be true? I had believed myself to be a champion of Light throughout the ages. How could I have also been the embodiment of pure darkness?

In response to this deep, riveting contemplation, a beam of ineffable light pierced through every resistance that I held onto. Mary Magdalene was touching me with the light of *forgiveness* and *compassion*. It melted all perceptions of pain, blame, and shame.

She began to telepathically show me all that had been, from a divine state of awareness. *My participation in the dark had always been in service to the light.*

My heart had never abandoned the greatest truth, and I had never denied my soul's essence. I had bravely stepped into the shadows of forgetfulness so that I could represent a darkness that was so genuinely needed upon the earth plane at that time.

This understanding shocked me.

Although I was able to sense its truth, it was not easy for me to believe that there is ever a valid reason for the tragedy that we have known. But Mary Magdalene continued to explain the deeper mysteries of this world so that I could bring peace to the parts of me that were feeling wounded by it all.

She revealed a broader view of our human existence. One that perpetually maintains a fundamental balance between all that is light and all that is dark—without any sense of battle existing between the two. There was always an intelligent life-force creating space for individual souls to see themselves as the victor, the savior, the peacemaker, and the wise one, as need be, for the collective growth and ascension of all humanity.

But in order for any one of us to discover our greatest potential, there must be a sense of believable duality in play, even if that duality is built upon illusion only.

Throughout time, every great victor has needed an imposing foe to push them beyond the bounds of comfort they had once known. And every valiant warrior for righteousness has needed a protagonist to make his cause worth fighting for. It's all a dramatic display of universal harmony and balance, in full array.

However, if every great being of light requires a contrasting catalyst upon this earth plane, which souls deserve to continuously walk in the light and which souls deserve to continuously walk in the shadows? If we were to participate in only one of these paths, we would be creating separation between our Self and the totality of our own infinite nature.

We all come from the same source. By accepting only one expression of truth over another, we are essentially denying an authentic part of our Self.

But, generally speaking, this is actually the dynamic that we have currently created for ourselves upon the earth plane. We all have very strong opinions of what behaviors we should or should not participate in—to the degree that there is punishment and shame for all inappropriate behavior.

These beliefs, as rational and righteous as they appear, are actually creating more and more separation between us. Although our actions can align with dark and shadowed energies, our souls can never "be" anything less than light.

Our whole concept of unworthiness is distorted. Every soul is equally worthy of love, joy, peace, abundance, grace, and acceptance—*including our own.*

The judgment we have placed upon ourselves and upon others is merely perpetuating an ever-expanding cycle of disempowerment, separation, and unworthiness.

It benefits no one.

This cycle needs to complete itself so that genuine healing can begin to take place within the heart of each precious soul that lives.

When Mary Magdalene held her hand out to welcome me home, it was to welcome me back into my own sacred and divine knowing. It was time to remember who I truly am, beyond all perceptions of shadow and pain, so that the healing could begin.

This heightened state of awareness triggered a profound vision of my soul, as it was, just moments before I incarnated into my first shadowed lifetime. I shone brightly with the same ineffable light that I had just witnessed in Mary Magdalene a few moments before.

My heart had always been pure! Even when I knew that I would soon forget who I was.

Upon the highest planes of sacred awareness, I had always wished to be of service to the Light and all that supported humanity's growth and evolution.

I clearly sensed that in order for humanity to discover its own innate power and force, it had required an antagonist of the darkest variety. By volunteering to be that antagonist, I would be encouraging countless souls to stand up for their own sacred empowerment. I would ignite the light within them, encouraging them to awaken from their own complacent slumber.

By embodying the dark, I was giving space for the light to grow in inconceivable measure.

Whether the light actually awakened in every soul, in that moment, was not my responsibility or my primary concern. As a wise master myself, I knew that gifting them the opportunity to set themselves free was my only priority and purpose.

In order to do that, without holding back, I had to commit to the energy I had volunteered to embrace. In order to authentically represent the darkness, I had to believe that I was the darkness. I had to forget who I was at deeper vibrations of truth.

And that is precisely where "the fall" took place in my own consciousness.

My crippling sorrow and pain hadn't come from merely participating in the darkest aspects of life. It had come from believing that participating in the darkest aspects of life would somehow separate me from my greater eternal truth.

At some point, I had judged the light to be more worthy and honorable than its shadowed counterpart, and I had judged myself for participating in that which was less than worthy and honorable.

As I stated earlier in this chapter:

> *These experiences never need to define our journey or negate the magnificence of all we are. Through every shadowed experience that may be, we remain connected to the boundless Light that is.*

Through every shadowed (and darker than dark) moment, experience, and lifetime, our soul remains pure and pristine.

Because divine awareness honors all free expression—without bounds, conditions, or limitations—we can never be any less than the Light we authentically are.

Through all varieties of experience on the physical planes of awareness, our eternal Light remains constant and immutable—*untouched by the shadows we have known.*

This awareness reminds me of this lifetime's most epic soul relationship; the one that propelled me into the unexpected depths of loss and despair.

In my innocence, I fell deeply in love with someone who appeared to be my everything. This beautiful soul was my anchor to beauty, love, and security in the world, never allowing me to feel alone.

In his embrace, I was home. Without ever needing to explain myself, I felt "seen." I felt understood.

I was 24 years old when we made all the worldly vows that two lovers often embrace, including vows of marriage, fidelity, and life-long commitment.

We then allowed life to carry us forward, seemingly as one. Through all of life's many adventures, we were the unshakable core.

I hold memories of disagreements that would melt away by us simply holding each other in a gentle embrace. But there were no mounting conflicts; nor hints to explain what would one day take place.

This man allowed me to be myself, without ever asking me to be any more. He spoke of our future and all that would lead us towards the edge of time, together. And then, without explanation, he abandoned that future and decided to not come home.

Our son was only six months old.

We had been married for eight years. But now those years felt empty and dark. *I couldn't see the light.*

My son became the center of my focus and attention. He brought inconceivable measures of joy, love, and inspiration to my life.

As a mother, I was as fully present and available as I could possibly be. I sought to fill his precious life with wide-eyed wonder and possibility. Laughter, too, was always an integral part of our reality.

But beneath the surface, where no one could plainly see, I was lost in the depths of my own despair.

Outwardly, I was the person who smiled and cared. But inwardly, I felt without hope and direction.

This is the moment I spoke of at the beginning of this book. This is the experience that shattered my world and threw me into a tailspin of disbelief.

It's also the exact moment that catapulted me forward into my own soul's awakening.

You see, if I had not plunged into that depth of pain and sorrow, I never would have discovered the immutable truth and power within me. This is my origin story! It is the beginning of all I soon would discover myself to be.

When he left, I wasn't feeling abandoned because he had decided to leave a relationship. I was feeling betrayed because this behavior was the exact opposite of all he had ever revealed to me.

This was the behavior of someone I didn't know.

His choice made me question who I was.

How could I have loved someone who could be this cruel? How could I have not seen the signs? How could I ever trust myself again?

These raw, open-ended questions were the exact same ones that led to my first communications with God and Source.

Without my struggle to understand the deeper truth, I would never have opened my awareness to see my world differently. His leaving, exactly as he did, was perhaps the most selfless gift he could have given me.

Of course, it's not always easy for me to see it that way. We, as human beings, are sensitive to a million different moments of insight and emotional candor. But when I am very clear about it all, I confidently know that the love we shared was pure and true.

In fact, if the love was not pure and true, it would not have caused me to search for greater understanding and purpose in life. For all to lead me into new planes of existential awareness, we both had to devote ourselves to the roles we had played, just as we had played them.

I often marvel at the love he must have for me, on the soul level, to have devastated me so completely on this physical realm. *Ultimately, he knew that I couldn't know myself until he pushed me to question myself.*

But there is another reason I am choosing to share this story now.

There is another unacknowledged facet to this tale of empowerment. When he chose to turn his back on the love that he had known, he took on mountains of guilt and shame. So much so, that he won't allow himself to welcome love and compassion into his life again.

We are accepting that I am now the radiant soul I am because he was brave enough to play that part for me. But now he has become attached to feeling unworthy of blessings, forgiveness, and love—and so he continues to perpetuate that cycle of guilt, shame, and unworthiness for himself.

The pure love that was so much a part of his spirit is now buried beneath years of mounting self-judgement and denial.

How many of us do this exact same thing? How often do we hold ourselves eternally accountable for the shadowed choices of our past?

Every new moment is fresh and full of potential, but we don't always allow ourselves to move through each cycle of growth and expansion to the end. Sometimes we are so consumed by the doubt of our worthiness, or the fear of what might come, that we neglect to welcome in the freedom, peace, and healing that brings in a new beginning.

> *"You are still facing your shadows, one by one, so that you may learn to embrace your light without limitation or fear. That is what is happening now. You stand upon this precipice of transmutation so that you can either trust in the truth you know to be real— or you can bow to the illusion that draws you near."*

> ~ Divine Spirit

Life is an enchanted unfolding, uniquely different for each soul who breathes.

This is why *personal discernment* is so valuable to one who is sensing their way through life. Only *we* can authentically know what resonates most for ourselves.

With each new stage and cycle of growth, truth remains constant for one who is comfortable in their own skills of masterful discernment.

> *"The precipice, between truth and illusion, can only be daunting for one who hesitates and doubts themselves."*

> ~ Divine Spirit

CHAPTER FOURTEEN

Cycles of Life

"All life lies in support of your soul's extraordinary journey into wholeness. Allow yourself to appreciate the growth that comes from each experience that pushes you to new heights of awareness. In truth, would you be who you are now, without both the struggles and the blessings?"

~ Divine Spirit

There is something to be learned, remembered, understood, or accepted in every nuance of life that purposely appears. However, there is no predestined path for all that flows. There is a flexibility and fluidity to all life-force, which justly implies that all things are continuously shifting and changing.

All life perpetually moves forward in a natural cycle of birth, death, and rebirth. The sun rises and falls. The oceans ebb and flow. And we rhythmically breathe, in and out, as each of our cells reaches its own moment of transformation, release, and renewal.

All life is creating itself anew, over and over again, holding onto only that which continues to support its evolutionary journey forward.

When one life experience is complete, it will naturally release itself to the eternal flame of divine consciousness and return to its original state of formless life-force potential. In its place, new life is created and sustained, for as long as it may support all who are participating in that experience.

To simplify these words, let's accept that as our inhale comes into fullness, it must surrender itself to become the exhale. By accepting that its own life path is full and complete, the inhale allows a graceful transformation to take place. It has traveled its path and has served its purpose. It now surrenders itself to the cycle of death, so that one form of life can miraculously lead to the next. Renewing itself, through the birth of the exhale, it continues forward without resisting the natural flow that brings balance and order to all life.

Every form of life is offered the same opportunity to transform itself in harmony with the divine flow. Every thought, action, intention, opportunity, and relationship live by the same natural decree. *Once it reaches its unique stage of fullness, it must surrender to some form of transformation that will allow it to experience life through a new form.*

When we find ourselves holding onto some element of life that has reached its natural stage of fullness, then we are holding onto something that no longer has space to grow, expand, and evolve. And if something is not growing, it's only surviving.

Can you sense that you might currently be holding onto some belief systems that are stuck at this stage of resistance and stagnation?

We often resist our soul's evolutionary growth because we are afraid of what comes next.

I've done this many times myself. I rationalize how to make challenging situations work because I'm fearful of what the unknown future might bring. If we are honest with ourselves, we all do this—with jobs we are tired of, relationships that bring more stress than kindness, and hopes that we are afraid to believe in.

But our discomfort actually comes from holding onto something that is no longer alive and thriving. It's time to let those experiences find peace and completion at that stage of awareness, so that we can positively focus upon all that they have the potential to evolve into.

It's important to note, at this point, that we are not suggesting that the thought, action, intention, opportunity, or relationship must come to a final end in order to balance itself out and honor the divine flow. *It may only be a shift in perception, shape, or form that is needed.*

For example, if our job becomes a bit uncomfortable, it could simply mean that we are ready for new levels of growth within that job or career. We may simply need to reflect upon the current perceptions, expectations, and goals that we hold in relation to that job or career—and make changes accordingly.

We might decide to accept new responsibilities, to bravely speak our truth, or to compassionately create new boundaries. By releasing from our old views and perceptions of limitation, we create space for the transformation and expansion to take place gracefully.

As one view of our potential reality completes itself, we allow another to birth itself.

And even if a job, experience, or relationship is brought to a final and unexpected end, it creates space for something new and extraordinary to powerfully appear.

As a fact, that job, experience, or relationship could not have ended if there was still more to learn and benefit from. It

could only complete itself because it was actually complete—
and your soul was ready for growth.

All change, unexpected or not, can be graceful and easy, when
we focus upon the positive expansion that is undeniably
taking place at some level.

It's important to be gentle with yourself. Feel your way
through each new moment of shift and change, without any
attachment to what "should" be or any fear of what "could"
be.

By remaining focused upon the growth and expansion that
will surely lead us through each purposeful transition in our
lives, we remain open to all currently available paths of
opportunity and support, without resistance.

> *"Let your soul discover the depths of its
> own infinite nature by dancing freely
> through all of life's many variations.
> Explore as fully as you dare to, trusting
> that each of life's boundless forms has its
> time and its place. All sacred experience is
> available to one who is willing to trust in
> the divine flow to gracefully carry them
> through each moment of transition and
> transformation."*

~ Divine Spirit

These powerful words encourage us to bypass our mind's
programmed insecurities, doubts, and fears, by inspiring us
to see all life, and its many variations, as opportunities to
discover something new and wondrous about ourselves.

These words even suggest that there is purpose to all unique
experience. But when one form of experience has outlived its
time, the *divine flow*—as an intelligent force of universal

169

consciousness—will naturally carry us forward to the next if we bravely trust in it to do so.

Even when we are unable to clearly see what comes next, we are being supported through each cycle of purposeful birth, death, and rebirth, as fully as we allow ourselves to be.

Now, let's go even deeper.

This fundamental understanding of the cycles of life will also help us to dispel every debilitating perception of illusion, shadow, struggle, and lack that may trigger us from time to time. In recognizing that every intimidating illusion has the ability to powerfully transform itself, we can find peace and empowerment in the darkest of places.

> *"It's easy for you to accept that all things can change in the blink of an eye, but have you ever considered that all things can be created in the blink of an eye?"*

> ~ **Master Merlin**

We hold the power to initiate all shift, change, and creative solution when we are ready to do so. Which rightly suggests that we never have to remain in any uncomfortable condition or situation if we don't wish to. Even our conscious thoughts alone, have the ability to alter our experiences at a core foundational level.

It's time to embrace the concept of "change" as a positive experience in our lives. Because, ultimately, all change is progressive, forward moving, and open to our suggestive influence.

Some of us stubbornly resist all forms of change because we innocently see change as being uncertain and unpredictable. But this resistance is motivated only by an irrational fear. I say "irrational" because the future has not yet been created. Any sense of challenge or uncertainty regarding change can, therefore, only be assumed; and only our positive focus has the potential to shift a perception of vulnerable uncertainty to one of inspired potentiality.

Change is inevitable because all Life, by its very definition, is most genuinely alive and in motion. But each inevitable change is also filled with opportunity for remarkable expansion and growth. *Change, itself, does not define our experience.* It's how we participate in, or react to, each subtle and epic change that directly shapes our reality.

For example, an unexpected rainbow might inspire us to see our day differently. But a bit of unexpected traffic might potentially do the same. Even though it's possible to see the traffic as an imposition, it's also possible to see it as an inspiration for redirection or re-evaluation.

I speak from experience. One of my greatest emotional clearings actually came through because of an unexpected traffic jam one ordinary afternoon.

At the time, I had been processing waves of repressed anger that had been unexpectedly rising to the surface. Each time the uncomfortable emotion emerged from within, I honored it and did my best to heal it, in love. I knew these were ancient energies that just needed to express themselves.

However, the anger kept returning. And this anger was beginning to feel more than emotional. It was becoming quite visceral, encouraging my body to feel disrespected and trapped. So, when I found myself physically stuck and unable to move forward in the traffic that suddenly appeared, I was deeply triggered.

I sensed a new measure of uncensored rage rising from within. And when I attempted to honor it, as I had done each time before, I became overwhelmed. I suddenly realized, while still stuck in the uncompromising traffic, that I held an entire ocean of repressed anger within me!

For a moment, I was deeply discouraged. How do I even begin to heal "an ocean" of anger? But with that genuine question came support from divine source. I heard these powerful words echo through my soul:

"With an Ocean of Compassion."

In my mind's eye, the skies had opened to shower a golden light upon all that I had imagined the ocean of anger to be. The light instantly healed all that was in disharmony. The healing was complete!

It was that easy. I could no longer resonate with the anger, injustice, and hopelessness that had affected me just a few moments before.

Of course, to be clear, the traffic was not responsible for that miraculous healing. It only served as an opportunity for me to feel disrespected and trapped, so that I could be honest about the emotions I had been repressing for so long.

At some level, I was ready to face those shadowed perceptions in a new way. So, this time, when the anger rose, I went deeper into it, without resisting the change and transformation that could potentially take place.

I acknowledged the rage and knew that there was no one else to blame for its existence. *All that I was holding within was my own creation.*

I was the one who identified with each individual story of pain and blame. And I was the one who had continued to hold this ocean of anger in place. If there was to be change, I would have to initiate it by knowing that I was ready to welcome change in.

And that is exactly what happened.

By simply removing my resistance (existing in the forms of denial and shame), I gave the anger permission to complete its own natural life cycle.

Compassion was, and is, a natural healing agent for all forms of anger. So, without understanding the power I held, I called that compassion from the higher planes of divine consciousness, to bring new life to the anger I was ready to release and transform.

Amazingly, it took only moments to finally release attachment to all that had taken countless lifetimes to amass. This aptly suggests that the original sensations of "anger" were most probably sensations I could have bravely faced and honored when they had first appeared.

I had believed that those emotions were too daunting to face, so they became too daunting to face.

We always hold the power to overcome and rise above each challenge that might present itself, but we may never recognize the power we hold if we are unwilling to bravely face the challenges that appear.

No challenge is ever so great that it changes the fundamental understanding of who we are. And yet, each time we believe that an external circumstance has the power to directly define our reality, we surrender to that implied perception of reality, without taking the time to acknowledge its deep potential to shift and transform.

I fell into a depression, so many years ago, because I had innocently surrendered to the fear-based illusions that proposed a relentless series of defeatist scenarios. I had not yet accepted that beyond the veil of separation and forgetfulness, my safety and security was constant and absolute.

As my awareness lifted, though, I learned to use the following mantra to remind me of my greater truth. It gave space for every one of my limiting thoughts to effectively fall away. And in their place, newly inspired thoughts became apparent and clear. This gracefully allowed for empowered transformations to take place.

"It's impossible for me to not be supported and blessed!"

I call it a "mantra," but it was simply the immutable truth of my soul, being repeated over and over. It brought me back to center, every single time, and helped me to see through every sticky point of illusion and fear. I still use it regularly, whenever something completely unexpected and potentially traumatic appears.

But there is a vital component to this mantra that must be accepted before all can gracefully align and find balance. We must accept that there is, most certainly, a supportive way through—without holding any attachment to what that supportive way must be.

In order for us to welcome new measures of support and love into any particular situation, we may need to look at the entire circumstance with fresh eyes. We may need to release from something that was considered important to us, or to accept something that we were wishing to avoid.

If we are not willing to change our outlook for all that is presenting itself, we will continue down the old familiar path of perceived challenge and conflict without ever acknowledging that other paths of opportunity already exist—or, at least, have the potential to exist.

Ultimately, I am wishing to instill a foundational belief that accepts, beyond compromise, that we always hold the power to shift, change, and redirect our experience, if we wish to do so.

If we truly are sacred and divine beings with infinite potential and power, then every perception of limitation, challenge, and struggle is but a *purposeful illusion.*

Sometimes we interpret the word "illusion" to carry a tone of manipulation and deviousness within; but this is untrue. We must fully accept an illusion as no more than "a state of limited awareness." It allows us to perceive some form of truth as the highest form of truth, without ever revealing that there is more to see.

But how do we discern whether the truth we currently trust in is illusion or not? How do we recognize an illusion if all illusions are designed to charm us into believing that "their truth" is the only truth?

> *"It's our own passionate Spirit that breaks ties to all perceptions of illusion and separation. In the presence of our own heart, we discover the undeniable truth of all that is love, seen and unseen. Without explanation or validation, we most certainly know."*
>
> ~ **Divine Spirit**

This is vitally important to me.

Discerning truth, for myself, is the only way I can feel comfortable in all of the many choices I make each day. But there was a time that I was so afraid to trust my instincts and intuitions as true and accurate that I lacked confidence in many of my choices. I was creating doubt and fear where there didn't need to be any.

I was definitely doing this in my earthly life. But even more concerningly, I was also doing this in my communications with Spirit and Source. I wasn't confident in all that was flowing through. I was even entertaining the idea of shutting down my gift of clear sight, to protect myself from false insights and channelings.

The irrational fears were mounting.

During one of the many uncomfortable bouts of confusion and self-doubt that I often experienced towards the beginning of my journey, I searched for clarity and inspiration. My soul was asking deep questions—and I was ready for answers.

What if I was imagining everything that felt so real? Or, even worse, what if I was trusting some energies that weren't worthy of being trusted?

It was the gentle presence of Blessed Mother that answered my prayer for greater understanding and truth.

With just a bit of light-hearted indulgence in her voice, she seemed to empathize with my fear, confusion, and distrust. She gently whispered, *"It must be horrible. What has been said to scare you so?"*

That question made me think more clearly.

Telepathically, I responded to her inquiry and told her that each spiritual guardian had spoken of my greatness and my empowered potential. They each had complimented me and treated me with immense kindness.

With power in her voice, this time, she simply asked:

"Then why would you close the door on love?"

Wow! That's profound.

Blessed Mother was speaking to me about so much more than the few channeled messages I had been receiving. She was speaking about the whole of Life, in all its grand existential beingness.

If I could learn to trust the energy of authentic Love to guide my way forward, I would never need to blindly place my faith into anything or anyone outside of myself.

Because I had essentially been taught to distrust the world around me, my restless mind had been entertaining a plethora of irrational fears. My consciousness had already risen enough to understand that those prejudiced beliefs were not necessarily relevant anymore, but they were still shaping the way I saw all new moments.

Blessed Mother was now offering me an opportunity to connect directly to the energies behind all that flows, instead of focusing solely on the appearance of all that is implied and suggested.

In other words, I was able to look beyond someone's defensive outburst, shy demeanor, innocent mistake, or obsessive behavior. I was able to recognize the motivation beneath all that appeared to be "true" on the surface.

Sometimes, in looking deeper, I recognized an innocent intention to love purely. Each soul was simply expressing themselves in the only way they knew how. And sometimes, I sensed that there was no kind and beautiful intention beneath the surface.

Let's be honest. Sometimes people only want to manipulate circumstances for their own benefit.

And that's perfect for their personal experience. *Their choices are not reflective of my worth.* Without any sense of judgment, I can honor their truth and love them as they are (as best as I can in each real and authentic moment).

However, I don't have to dance with them if I don't wish to. I never have to share my precious life-force energy with those who don't inspire me or respect me.

Blessed Mother was teaching me to *witness the truth* of all interpersonal communications, without judging them.

With this approach, I wouldn't need to understand every intimate detail of someone's life in order to sense whether I could trust them, personally. I only needed to sense whether the energy they shared with me, in each individual moment, was genuine and filled with a loving intention.

Were they being *authentic* and *honest* with themselves and with me?

This knowledge gave me the power to confidently make choices for myself without righteously judging "who they are" and "who they have been" on some grand scale of arbitrary assumption.

I used this new approach objectively, for every relationship in my life, regardless of how trivial or precious each relationship was.

The results were beautiful and unexpectedly freeing.

I learned to love more fully.

Sensing someone by their energy, alone, allowed me to fall deeply in love with strangers who I would never meet again. It also enabled me to create compassionate space between myself and those I had known for years, when needed.

Creating healthy boundaries helps us to remain focused on vibrations of love and support, instead of vulnerability and defense.

I was learning to witness the deeper truths that were always available to someone who was willing to let love guide the way. This was an epic shift in awareness for someone who had been feeling powerless and perpetually confused.

I no longer needed to understand everything about everything. I only needed to become aware of what was directly related to my current experience. And if something felt, energetically, like it was less than loving and supportive, I gave myself permission to *redirect my focus* to something that was more inspirational and uplifting.

Can you sense the simplicity in this?

I'm not speaking solely about relationships any longer. This practice of "choosing love" became a core component of my *foundational truth*—that which all else is built upon.

There was no longer anything to battle or protect myself from because it was just a matter of choice. Every thought, every opportunity, and every candid experience offered me an opportunity to "choose love," again and again.

But clearly, we all understand that love isn't always easy to recognize; especially when we are in the midst of our own chaos, confusion, or pain. Sometimes we need to sense it, intuitively, in those bright spaces that exist beyond our perceptions of chaos, confusion, and pain.

I continuously remind myself that if love is not apparent in any particular moment, then it is my privileged right to connect to it upon the unseen planes that authentically exist. I never have to accept less than I am worthy of.

Simply said, love is always present! Even when it's hidden and unseen. I just have to find it, wherever it might be.

With this awareness, I am no longer bound to only that which *appears* to be true. If love—in the form of inspiration, joy, peace, kindness, or support—cannot be found upon one path of discovery, I can look for it upon another. Which, thereby, allows me to face the barrage of intimidating illusions that life sometimes throws at us without losing my confident focus and enlightened awareness.

We are acknowledging, upon a massive scale of infinite potential and possibility, that our blessed and supported journey is constant and immutable. We are no longer surrendering to the perceptions of proposed challenge and trauma that merely "appear." We are, with compassionate grace, finding our own empowered way through each intimidating crossroad that may present itself.

Focusing on positive and loving energies also suggests that we are focused upon all that is life-giving, forward moving, and expansive in our life—which guarantees our connection to the divine flow and all that is evolving naturally through the cycles of birth, death, and rebirth.

If we are constantly focused upon all that is affirmative, we can effortlessly allow that which is complete and without space for growth to naturally transform into newly expanded paths of discovery.

I cannot stress this point enough.

There is *always* more than we can see.

We have only ever felt weak, limited, disappointed, disempowered, or afraid because we didn't know that being happy and loved was an available option. We let the illusions of struggle and conflict stop us from seeing the greater potential that can be.

We let "life" bully us into feeling disempowered and without choice. But there is always *more* for one who is ready to accept "more" into their life.

If we remember that every shadowed perception and purposeful illusion can transmute into love with our confident focus and enlightened awareness, then we become the empowered masters of our own blessed journeys.

We become the architects of all that creatively births itself in support of our sacred experiences.

When we are willing to let all that is uncomfortable, hollow, and inert fall away, we create space for all that is our *chosen fate.*

This is an oxymoron, I know. But a perfectly expressed one, since only *we* have the power to shape our own fateful destiny.

> *"You must release attachment to your insecurities before you can step forward into the next cycle of growth. For they can all be removed, but if you do not release all personal resonance and attachment to them first, the peace you find will only be temporary. An end to all suffering cannot be found outwardly. It must be cultivated from within by choosing peace and love repeatedly."*
>
> **~Divine Spirit**

As we move through our cycles in life, it is vitally important to not just move through the motions of growth. If we believe that changing our circumstances will change our experiences, we are simply deluding ourselves. The motivation and intention behind each step forward must be pure.

Over and over, I have watched people choose a bright new path in life, and then carry all their past patterns and behaviors—the ones that had created challenge and conflict in the past—along with them.

Life will most generously offer us opportunities to begin again, as often as we are ready for that growth. But the freedom that we find in each new experience can only be found when we see ourselves truly beginning again.

Change must take place at all levels of awareness.

Are you willing to believe that you are worthy of a new beginning? Are you ready to release all that no longer serves your journey forward?

These important questions place energy into motion. They clear the path for all that resonates and aligns with you in each new moment. Because, remember, your future is not yet created. It will always shape itself to honor all that is comfortable for you.

In other words, you will only recognize the opportunities that personally resonate with you.

Once, I was supporting a friend through an epic move. She was searching for a new space to call "home." But I noticed that she was willing to settle for much less than she was worthy of. I recognized this pattern because I had done this exact thing myself many times before.

This time, however, I was able to witness the limited patterns of thought that held her back from so much more than she could see. In support of her healing and growth, I intuitively heard these powerful words echo through:

*"Are you a refugee of your past traumas or
an inheritor of a new reality?"*

There is a world of difference between the two.

So often, we want the freedom that lies ahead, but we are simultaneously holding on to all the past trauma, insecurities, and pain we have known. In these cases, we are seeking to escape our past life experiences by changing no more than the outer world.

However, something extraordinary happens when we realize that we have already grown. At fundamental levels within, we are no longer who we used to be. We can no longer resonate with the same conflict, disharmony, or disrespect we had resonated with before, so our experiences will truly be new and expansive, if we trust them to be.

This is essentially what we are all searching for; the freedom to start again so that we might explore new measures of boundless joy. But, to be clear, that freedom is already ours! *We are the catalysts for all epic change and inspired growth.* It can be no other way.

I encourage you, passionately, to trust in who you already are.

The cycles of life, growth, and expansion are always in motion, offering us opportunities to begin again. They will carry us forward, with ease and grace, when we are focused on all we are ready to confidently embrace.

The changes we seek, for them to be genuine and pure, must initiate from within.

We must recognize that we are the center of it all.

Chapter Fifteen

Humanity's Evolution

"In this lifetime, you will shatter the perceived limitations of your humanity. You will welcome the fullness of all you are upon the higher planes of consciousness into your human form, thereby ushering in a whole new paradigm of existence for humankind. Let yourself dream, wildly. For you are the gift that this world most requires now. Allow yourself to believe in all that can be."

~ Divine Spirit

These words are being spoken to each of us directly. It reminds us that we each carry a unique spirit, fire, and light within; one that is allowing divine source to express itself in fresh new ways.

We were never created to follow the path that is already known and explored, in the same way that has already been known and explored before. There would be no growth in that experience. We are here, in our own perfect ways, to breathe a new breath and to chart a new course.

This excites me!

We're being offered an opportunity to create a world of our own imagining—one that never has to be "colored inside the lines."

This idea reminds me of the words a wise earth guardian recently shared with me in Spirit. I was at the Oregon coast when it happened. I had been admiring the scenery just a few miles north of the California border when I intuitively sensed a sacred horn blowing to the right of my path. I sensed a group of ancient people watching my steps.

When I tuned into the higher plane of consciousness upon which this experience was happening, I sensed a wise elder step forward from the group. I'll call him Grandfather.

Grandfather walked with me and shared much insight about the first peoples of that land. They lived in harmony and peace, with great respect for the land and for the Light that lived within each sacred soul. They saw each child as a messenger from the higher realms; one that was born to bring greater balance to the world.

Grandfather showed me that when any energy was needed to help their people evolve, they prayed for that energy to be carried forward through the birth of a new child. And when that child arrived, they did not teach that child what to expect in the world that they were now a part of.

Instead, the elders of that clan created opportunities for that child to interact with Life in its own way. They led each child to the waters, as an example, and asked: *"What do you see? What do you sense? What do you feel?"*

With great appreciation and admiration for all that was intuitively sensed, they encouraged each child to create his or her own unique relationship to the world around them.

These children learned to look within for truth and wisdom. They learned to trust their own instincts and to value all that they naturally contributed to the collective experience that they were a part of. They did this while also acknowledging that every other soul contributed something of equal importance in their own unique way too.

This is the element of *human evolution* that has been forgotten. Not lost, mind you. Just forgotten.

Each of us contributes something of great value and purpose to the whole, whether we recognize it or not.

To truly understand this, we must understand our intimate connection to the whole. The "whole" cannot exist, as it is, without each and every one of us. It is, after all, a *collective* of every individual soul gathered into a single entirety, excluding no one.

This also suggests, correctly, that no one within the whole of the human collective can possibly have a greater impact upon the whole than any other. Every individual makes an equal contribution to the whole of "humanity."

This makes our assumptions of self-proclaimed insignificance, in relation to the current human condition, appear quite absurd. If we do not personally hold the power to affect compassionate change upon a global scale, who does?

Some of us have grown quite complacent in believing that others are responsible for all the conflicts that exist in our human collective. But every time we do this, we negate the power that we each hold upon the higher planes of unity consciousness. We're giving far too much energy to the physical condition alone.

I'm here to remind you that our conscious thoughts greatly impact the whole!

Our thoughts serve as discerning voices upon the purely conscious planes that energize and direct all life-force. And although our single voice sounds like no more than a mere whisper upon those planes of infinite magnitude and potential, it unites with every other single voice of similar and resonant belief.

These united voices, even in their silence upon the physical planes, are what powerfully inspire phenomenal waves of change and expansion on the energetic planes.

Imagine that each one of our silent prayers for peace and harmony unites with every other silent prayer for peace and harmony. And as our collective prayer becomes bolder and more confident, it creates space for manifest change upon the physical plane.

Even as we are focused upon our physical experience alone, we remain intimately connected to the energetic planes, where only pure consciousness thrives and directs all.

> *"Connect to the truth within your hearts! Our presence—as spiritual teachers, guardians, and elders—is only possible because it has been requested by you and others like you. As you welcome greater divine support and blessing, we respond, to gift you with remembrance of all you are. Your prayers, for greater insights and healing, open gateways of communication between your dimensional plane and our own."*

> ~ **Divine Spirit**

In order to honor humanity's free-will experience, only that which humanity wills into being may be known upon the earth plane.

This is why our voices make a difference.

We must be the ones to invoke greater healing, empowerment, and divine truth.

In 2009, I held a vision of strangers coming together in a sacred way. So, I invited people to gather on the beach, where we created large mandalas in the sand with the ancient limestone rocks that had recently washed up on that Florida beach. For four years, we did this for every equinox and solstice that passed.

I was innocent in my original intention. I couldn't possibly see the full scope of all that I was powerfully introducing into the earth plane. I only knew that I was creating an opportunity for those involved to remember their intimate and divine connection.

After one of these gatherings, I went back out to the beach to sit near the mandala we had recently built. I was amazed to see that the energy we had activated during our sacred ceremony was still alive and in motion. Every prayer we had invoked, for all humanity, was still holding true. I understood this because of a miraculous vision that was granted to me.

With my divine sight, I watched our mandala rise from the earth like a formidable shield of heavenly light and direct itself towards the heart of each soul upon that beach.

In essence, it presented itself to each soul and graciously asked, *"Would you like to receive this blessing?"* If a soul accepted the opportunity that was being offered, the shield of light merged into that soul's heart space. If a soul denied the opportunity, the shield of light happily redirected itself to the next soul who might be blessed.

It was phenomenal to watch. But ultimately, Spirit was trying to illustrate how our energy impacts all of humanity. Once we bring life to some form of creative energy, it exists as a potential opportunity for every soul who might be blessed.

I had created the physical gathering for the few who had joined us, but the benefits of my sacred intentions were reaching far beyond anything I had the ability to initially comprehend.

Imagine the same happening each time we offer kindness to one who is lost; or we offer love to a child who is growing. Our intentions are to solely support the one who stands before us, but our efforts are speaking to every soul who might be blessed.

With every act of kindness, compassion, and love, we are introducing the experience of kindness, compassion, and love into our human consciousness. We are offering all humanity an opportunity to share in each of these energies, if they so wish.

> *"For humanity to ascend beyond all perceptions of struggle and lack, we encourage you to first see yourself as empowered, then every other soul as empowered, and then all humanity as empowered. All shifts must begin within if they are to effectively reach throughout."*

> **~ Divine Spirit**

We cannot possibly inspire others to reach heights that we have not yet reached ourselves. If we are doubting our abundant security and boundless divine potential, we cannot yet lead others into those sacred mysteries.

This means that in order to walk with integrity and power, we must honor our own journey as a priority! It is the most generous thing we can do for ourselves and all humanity.

Wherever you are on your path towards greater enlightenment, it's important to authentically "be there."

Don't distract yourself from your own growth by focusing merely on the growth of others.

All global shift and change must begin within, in the purest ways. And sometimes the purest ways are also the simplest ways.

A breath that is breathed in love illuminates the world we are a part of.

> *"In holding the light purely within yourself, you become the beacon that inspires all humanity to remember their own greatest potential. Don't be afraid to shine brightly! Your light is the greatest gift you have to share."*
>
> ~ **Divine Spirit**

I always find great comfort in realizing that one small effort based in integrity, creates a much greater impact in our collective consciousness than any well-intentioned ideal ever could.

This thought allows me to be gentle with myself. I don't have to be the loudest voice or the boldest change-maker in order to affect powerful change.

I just have to be me.

By focusing on our own precious growth and soul expansion, we naturally contribute to the collective energy that supports all humanity.

Everyone wants to rise in their own way. Everyone wants to be inspired and live in love. By trusting that every precious soul has the power to create these experiences for themselves, we give them the opportunity to discover their own boundless potential.

We start with our own growth so that we can learn to believe in the extraordinary blessings that are perpetually available to all of us.

We effectively begin within, but we affect change throughout.

Too often we believe that others are powerless in their respective journeys. But we can no longer believe that we, individually or collectively, need to "be saved" from any traumatic reality because we are all equally empowered and free. The perception that we must be saved from some grand injustice is actually holding us back from exploring our soul's greatest, and always accessible, power and purpose.

For a moment, let's recall that I spent much of my life believing that I was a fierce warrior who needed to protect and save those who couldn't protect and save themselves. I was indoctrinated to believe that it was my duty, as a "good" person, to lift others from their ignorance, their struggle, and their pain.

And if we are honest with ourselves, we can acknowledge that this thought pattern is still common across our earth plane.

I only wished to love people. But by envisioning myself as a "savior," I was energizing their stories of victimhood, challenge, and pain. Even with my silent thoughts alone, I was supporting their disempowerment by feeling pity for their predicament or fear for their uncertain future.

This was helping no one. And, it was making it exceedingly hard to trust in the infinite blessings that Spirit was encouraging me to believe in.

I wanted to change this perception of unyielding victimhood and lack, but it was a struggle for me. Each time I tried to see someone in their power, it felt as though I was abandoning them in their current situation. It didn't feel like I was being very loving and supportive.

Spirit understood the dilemma that was pulling at my heartstrings, so they brought me an incredibly powerful vision to expand my understanding of truth.

In this vision, I found myself kneeling down, desperate, at the bottom step of a beautiful temple of ethereal Light. It felt as though this was a truly ancient time, one that precedes our recorded history.

From that place of surrendered desperation, I was beseeching those upon the top step within the temple of Light to help those who were suffering upon the earth plane. I felt the presence of faceless multitudes behind me, in the density of that earthly experience, calling out for support and assistance. My passionate prayers were to "save them" from their troubles and challenges.

It's quite important to note that I was not personally in discernable pain or struggle. I was not concerned with my own well-being. I was only focused upon the well-being of those who couldn't help themselves.

My vision then expanded. I was able to note that although my body appeared to be strewn upon the bottom step of that temple—far removed from all that was held so pure upon the top step—I was actually born into the energies of that pristine temple of Light.

Only a shift in consciousness allows me, at any time, to envision myself at either the bottom step or the top step—also symbolizing, more accurately, the two separate worlds of earthly matter and spiritual perfection.

I was envisioning a separation between the two realms of reality, so there was a separation. But even from the lowliest point of separation, I was directing my energy and prayers to the pristine part of myself that knew we were all one.

Bravely now, understanding that it's all a conscious construct, I imagined myself rising to the top step. I acknowledged that I held the power to support and assist every soul that might find themselves in need. But from the top step, I was no longer able to identify with their stories of lack and injustice. I knew that they all held the power to effortlessly rise when they were ready to do so.

I began to call out to each one, *"I see you! I see your beauty, your potential, and your pristine nature."*

In response, I saw them wanting to believe me.

They needed someone to see what they couldn't see within themselves. They needed a brilliant force of inspiration, encouragement, and hope to light the way through any shadowed moments that may be.

This helped me, profoundly.

I realized that humanity doesn't need someone to support them in their victimhood; *they need someone to believe in their empowerment.*

So, now, even in the darkest of times, I strive with a bold determination to be a beacon of compassionate hope and enlightened truth.

You and I are active contributors to the human collective. It may seem as though our silent prayers, in the face of great conflict and chaos, are inconsequential and ineffective—but that is not true. They are ushering Light into the shifting tides of human evolution.

Be brave. Know that our empowered visions create an open path for others to also follow and embrace when they are ready to do so. They inspire minds to think differently than they once had, so that choices may expand beyond all that had previously been known.

Even if our visions do not appear to be understood by others, they create space for conscious expansion and exploration to take place. On a subtle level, change is being introduced and evolution is underway.

I think this is the element that often goes unacknowledged.

Once we introduce a new view of inspired potential, either individually or collectively, we change the fundamental framework of human potential. Our gentle suggestions become an available choice for all who would be blessed—and that changes everything.

We are the ones we've been waiting for!

We are the teachers, the prophets, the healers, the priestesses, the heroes, and the philosophers. We are the ones who are creating new paradigms of heart-centered being and free-spirited exploration. We must learn to trust ourselves and the power we hold within.

If you are one who can understand the words, spoken and unspoken, that are communicated in this book, then you are one of the enlightened ones—leading the way home to *Divine Self*.

First for yourself, then for every soul you meet.

Just by being the extraordinary and remarkable being you naturally are, without any need to be anything other than all you are, the direction of humanity's growth and evolution is profoundly altered.

Yes. You are that amazing!

"One day in your near future—a day with no distinguishing traits—you will see the world that you believe to know, as the transformable world of your hopes and dreams. Where light comes from within and peace touches all. This mighty day already approaches for many of you now. So, we encourage you to remember that each human day brings another new dawn and a new opportunity to see in new ways. The magic you embrace in your own precious life will inspire an expansion of beliefs and possibilities—both for yourself and those you meet. Be not afraid of what will be. For you are now the CREATORS of all you seek!"

~ **Divine Spirit**

We are awakening to recognize just how precious we already are. Through our mere presence—our essential beingness—we affect change and make a difference.

Can you, for a moment, see yourself and every soul that is, as a sacred and divine spark of light?

Imagine that spark as a pure flame of divine consciousness that can be as small and reserved or as fierce and magnificent as it wishes to be. This flame is not destructive; it's life-giving and creative.

When we doubt ourselves and question our purpose, this spark of light dwindles. It becomes diminished in the shadows of our insecurities. But when we trust ourselves and hold love in our hearts, it ignites itself into the brilliance of a thousand suns.

Can you sense the power in this imagery? We each hold the flame of divine consciousness within. We each hold the passionate fire of life-giving creation within. In our own way, each of us are keepers of this eternal flame—and we can be no less.

And what happens when one single spark of light lends itself to a willing material or form?

It spreads.

Quite early upon my journey, long before I understood the concept of divine consciousness or a sacred flame, I was gifted a life-changing dream vision—one of an illuminating nature. I couldn't begin to understand its symbolism, but I held securely onto the feeling of joy and excitement that the dream had awakened in me.

In this dream, there were rows of flickering candle flames floating before me. They mesmerized me, so I lifted my finger in curiosity. As my finger moved closer to the flame I had approached, that flame grew and expanded. It seemed as though it had responded to my innocent presence.

I had considered that reaction to be fun, as I recall. So, I picked another candle flame and repeated the same experience.

How interesting!

A "fire" of passionate joy ignited within me now. So, I opened my palm and directed it towards a grouping of small individual flames. The flames collectively expanded and danced in response to my playful movement.

This is when the excitement grew to new heights within my soul. I lifted both of my arms and edged them backwards, to allow for maximum impact, of course. With palms open and ready, I released them forward to watch the miraculous display appear.

Each individual flame had ignited itself to become one with every other flame. Each feeding the whole, giving birth to a Light that was now indefinable and boundless.

It was alive!

At a level that was pure, but inconceivable to the mind, my soul had been awakened from the slumber I didn't even know it was in. I awoke from that "dream" knowing that I make a difference—even when those differences are silent and unseen.

So do you!

You, and all that wondrously makes you who you are, is needed as no other can be needed. Our current world, in fact, is made up of the ripples and waves YOU have placed in motion.

Don't let this awesome truth concern you. I remind you that all Life exists in perfect balance. Your past contributions were perfect reflections of humanity's collective consciousness, in some way.

But if you're ready for change now, I encourage you to accept greater accountability for the energies you contribute to the whole. *You are the way humanity ascends beyond the concepts of chaos, and evolves into the realities of peace.*

You make a difference.

Become aware of your thoughts, actions, and efforts. Are they inspiring and uplifting? Do they create space for growth and expansion, or do they silently believe in a world that is doomed and inherently flawed?

Humanity needs us to believe in its power and its potential, now, more than ever before. It needs us to hold a vision of peaceful co-existence.

Will you join me in this?

When you are ready to see our world differently, your vision of what can be will effectively create shift and change in our mutual reality.

> *"Do not doubt the mystery that is you! You are the bridge between heaven and earth. You are the chalice, the vessel, and the conduit through which these two worlds unite. Through you, all is made whole. Trust yourself to effortlessly BE all you most naturally are.*
>
> *This is the moment you've been waiting for. Your awakening has already begun."*
>
> ~ **Divine Spirit**

CHAPTER SIXTEEN

Empowered Knowing

"It is time to reclaim your sacred mastery. Return to the vaults of treasured knowledge, to SEE that you are the Light of embodied divinity."

~ Divine Spirit

These words do not speak of the knowledge that can be found in a sacred book or revered teaching. These words speak of the wisdom held within your soul—the sacred truth that you have been safekeeping.

You have always known that you are divine and precious! You have always known that you are inexplicably connected to every extraordinary wonder that is and can be. It doesn't make sense to your logical mind; but still, you have always known. I do not doubt this.

All of our journeys, great and small, have led us towards discovery of this truth in physical form.

This is why we are mesmerized by a perfect rose, a colorful sunset, and a child's innocent smile. In these things, we sense the divine mystery. We sense that which is known but can never be fully understood through logic alone.

We are all searching for a validation that will remain elusive for as long as our divinity remains separate from our identity of Self. For it is only our *inner knowing* that can bring us the intangible proof and acceptance we crave.

Are you ready to trust yourself?

This can only be comfortable for those of us who are truly confident in the connection we hold within. For that is the knowledge that can never be lost, challenged, or taken away.

It is only our inner knowing that can bring us home to our *Divine Self.*

I am speaking, most certainly, of that which can only be known in your heart space—that space of purity and light within—where no fear or sense of duality can live because only immutable truth holds sway.

Our heart leads to completely different experiences than our mind leads us to. Fundamentally, the *mind* is no greater or less than the *heart*. But as a tool of navigation in our lives, it is different in every way. Our mind is a tool of logic and order. It works best when information makes "sense," within its scope of current awareness.

Spirit has taught me to see the mind as a vast and expansive library of knowledge. It has something to say about everything—but it can only contemplate that which it already has knowledge of. It's a space of stored information only. It can only access and acknowledge the knowledge, wisdom, and truth that we have previously accepted as "true and real."

Let's imagine, for a moment, that you have never felt the sensation of "cold" before. If you have never considered that the concept of "cold" existed, you would not have a stored understanding of what it is and what it represents. You would, when noticing it for the first time, sense that it was different than anything you had previously known. Then you would assign a description that makes sense to you; a description that generally represents the new sensation.

You might make correlations to contrasting or similar energies, or you might associate words and thoughts to the sensation that intuitively feels right. In essence, you are creating an imprint of what the energy of "cold" now means to you.

This imprint, or meaning, is now a way for you to validate the presence of cold in the future. But, ultimately, it was your heart—not your mind—that allowed you to sense the new sensation and create a new understanding to be stored away in your mind.

Our heart is the way we feel our way through life.

It speaks a language that is sensitive, adaptable, and relative. It needs no validation because it is its own source of intuitive truth and knowing.

This is the way of all enlightened teachings. We are taught to honor the information that comes through all paths of wisdom, including that which comes through the mind and every book of knowledge that the mind has ever created. But it can only be *the heart* that discerns truth in each simple and epic story that it hears. It's only the heart that can truly know something, beyond a doubt.

Even when that "knowing" is only fleeting, because all life is in constant motion, it is only the heart that can access the truest wisdom in each passing moment.

As life spirals into new expressions of boundless truth, it is our heart that allows us to feel safe, supported, and loved in each new moment. It is constantly attuning to all new vibrations of authentic truth.

You might even consider the heart to be fluid, like water. You can sense it, feel it, and know it—but to hold onto it is to stop its natural flow. In comparison to the water element, the mind would be immovable, like stone. Not because it cannot be moved; simply because it cannot move itself.

Each stone must be moved by some external force; redirected with purpose by nature or by man. The mind is the same way. If you'd like to change a belief, you must make the effort to change it. You must replace—or reprogram—one perception of truth with another that now holds greater resonance.

Only *you* can do this for yourself.

Life is continuously offering us opportunities to do this, but we will never trust the alternate truths that appear if we do not first trust ourselves to "know."

When contemplating the ending of this book, I began to place great pressure upon myself to sum up the mighty teachings of all previous chapters with something especially profound and wise. I stumbled through all the options my beautiful mind had suggested, until I silenced them all and took a break.

I sat outside beneath the full moon's light and simply asked to see. It was an innocent prayer that allowed me to look beyond everything I currently had an awareness of. It moved me outside the box I had placed myself within.

In that moment of surrender, I felt the intimate sensations of a past life vision coming through. I moved through each precious moment of awareness without remembering that I had asked "to see."

The vision began by me seeing myself as a very young girl, looking up to each soul who had professed great love for God and the Divine. I was enamored by the passionate faith they each knew. It was beautiful to watch and to witness.

But as I grew older, I started to see their "faith" more clearly. They were either speaking great truths without embodying the Light they spoke of, or they were speaking great lies as if they were God's truth.

I was becoming disillusioned in the disconnect that was now clear. I had seen each of these souls as brilliant and illustrious. Why were they becoming these empty vessels of false truth and inane prophecy? It made no sense to my own innocent mind.

With a faith that was pure within, I took it upon myself to remind each soul of the direct connection they had to divine source. I encouraged them to look deeper within and to trust truth for themselves. My desire was to restore them to the glory that I had once believed them to represent.

But as I passionately sought to empower them, my own radiance grew. Each time I tried to convince them of the magnificence that the divine represented within, my own love for the divine was growing exponentially.

I couldn't see, until it was too late, that their love of the divine was merely contrived. As much as they wanted to connect, through their words, prayers, and baseless acts of faith, they were only connecting to what their idea of God, Faith, and Love were. They couldn't sense the ineffable truth that lies beyond their own imposed assumptions.

All that I had witnessed in them, when I was young, was my own interpretation of truth reflected onto them. But in an epic reversal of fate, they were now witnessing their own interpretation of truth reflected onto me.

As my light grew brighter, they feared that light and deflected that fear through false prophecy. They persecuted me for the innocent light that was pure within.

In this vision, I felt the disappointment of speaking my truth and being persecuted for it. I felt the memories of pain and disappointment rise, until I understood why it had taken me so long to believe in this book, in this lifetime.

I began to work on the core outline of this book more than ten years ago. In each year, from then until now, I had fully believed that I would complete the book easily. But it has taken me more than ten years to believe in it—or more accurately—to believe in myself.

To the best of my ability, I have been living the life that I write about in these pages. However, by sharing it with the world, I open myself to a whole new realm of vulnerability that I had not understood before this vision.

As I remained surrendered under the full moon's light, my past life vision began to shift. I was now brought back to a dream that I had experienced near the very beginning of my journey, nearly 18 years ago. It was, perhaps, the first dream of epic proportion that had served to expand my awareness.

In this dream, I had come upon a large group of people casually gathered outside a large stadium. It felt as though I wasn't supposed to be there, so I tried to move my way through, as gently as I could. But everyone was generous of spirit and entirely welcoming. They invited me to sit at a large picnic table with them, and random conversations began to ensue, as they often do when meeting new acquaintances.

I joined in the conversations as if I had known this group my whole life. I was comfortable and at home. So, when their conversations led to spiritual curiosity, I confidently replied, *"God lives within."*

With those words, all conversations paused, and they collectively implored me to tell everyone. They passionately suggested that everyone must know this—and I must be the one to tell them.

I giggled and reminded them that everyone already knows this. But they assured me that this was not true. They felt strongly that I must be the one to tell everyone that God lives within.

Then, with an even greater sense of urgency in their voices, they suggested that I must go into the stadium and speak this truth.

I suddenly understood that the heads of all major religions were inside that stadium. They were discussing, and dictating, the mightiest precepts of "divine law." (Which is, of course an ironically comical pair of words from my current state of heightened consciousness.) But at the time of this dream I felt quite humbled by the authority of all those figures that must have been gathered in that stadium.

In a fateful duel of call and response, my beautiful new friends continued to assert, *"You must tell them!"* And I continued to respond, *"They already know."*

This continued back and forth—until I changed the rhythm of it all.

In that perfect moment, when my ego surrendered all I thought I knew, I silenced myself to go within. I closed my eyes and asked the voice of my own sacred soul to guide me forward.

I came out of that silence with the simplest of words— carrying the greatest of power.

I proudly exclaimed, *"Yes, I will."*

I instantly awoke from the dream at that point and continued on with my ordinary life. I knew the vision had been special, but I never understood the symbolism and power of it all until that night, nearly twenty years later, under the full moon's light.

With both the past life vision and the memory of this dream experience, all became clear. The truth of my soul was laid out before me.

I have always held a sacred connection to the Divine, in this lifetime and all those lives that had come before. My heart has always been enamored by those who intimately and purely know God's eternal love. But it was now time to go outside my comfort zone and speak my sacred truth.

There were no more bounds to contain the concepts of God, Love, and Divine Truth. There was only an acceptance of all that was pure and true for each soul, uniquely.

I understand.

"God lives within."

There is no separation between "all that is" and "all that I am." So I trust myself to speak my truth; a truth that has been waiting eons to be expressed without censor.

As my dream outside the stadium had suggested, I accept that my place is *outside* the "official forums" of spiritual communication and religious law. And I am proud of that beautiful place!

I have no need of walls, doctrines, relics, sacrifice, or false proxies. I stand here, in my own little space of boundless being, speaking my truth with the simplest of words.

I have faith that these words will gracefully find those who are ready to trust their own inner knowing too.

Because, in all truth:

"God lives within."

Never were truer words spoken. Only, these words are so much more expansive than I ever could have imagined when I first heard them.

They do not speak of the God we've known in any religious tradition. They speak of the sovereign light and authority of our own precious *Divine Self*.

I had, essentially, accepted the call to spread this message because I was intimately acquainted with the darkest of dark nights. I was tired of revering the promises of a "salvation" that could never come—because every form of salvation would still tether me to a perception of victimhood and lack. The word itself implied that I needed saving, thereby perpetuating my disempowerment in a world that was truly filled with *potential* and *possibility*.

I was ready to take my power back.

Dependent upon no other, I was ready to see my way through each perception of limitation that appeared. Which, of course, is the story that I've shared with you here.

But I must be exceedingly clear now.

Your story is powerful in its own right! Your story is unique and has a message that is profound and purposeful.

Never compare the brilliance of YOU to all that you perceive outwardly. Go within to sense your own valuable and worthy truth.

I could no longer assume that the knowledge I held within— although accessible to all—was actually known or accepted by all. It was now safe to speak my inherent truth without fear of retribution and condemnation. The memories of persecution are behind me.

It is time to spread my messages of free thought, clear sight, and direct connection. Perhaps you sense a passionate drive to spread your own messages of truth too.

I encourage you to do so, in love.

Our divine connection can no longer be defined by any set of dogmatic principles. For we are the only ones who can authentically know what feels right for us in each new moment of soul exploration.

We are the only ones with direct access to our unique understanding of the divine!

We must each find ways to cultivate and trust in this truth for ourselves. Through the thoughts we embrace, the acts we participate in, and the realities we create, we must be the ones to light the way as only we can.

In that dream at the stadium so many years ago, I accepted my role as a Divine Channel and Sacred Visionary in this world—without ever understanding what that truly meant.

I was naturally guided forward, to represent those energies as best as I was able. But, by finishing this book, in this very moment, I am giving voice to the purest parts of my divine nature.

I am finally ready to accept all that I most genuinely am.

Without needing any validation from the world around me, I am ready to sing my song and be heard. I pray that the love I hold in my heart is known in ways that only the purest of hearts can discern. For I stand here now, as the mighty soul who has walked through all Time and Space.

I do remember!

All is now clear.

I see myself being no more than Light. I sense my bright spirit wanting to love more fully. I remember volunteering for this life and every other life that I have ever lived.

I see the wisdom that I have carried through the ages, and I am in awe of all that I am proudly sharing now.

Trust that these words can serve as portals to expansive worlds of unexplored mysteries—if you find yourself inspired to dive that deeply into them.

Do not focus so intently upon my truth that you neglect to marvel upon your own truth. For it's so very clear! You have walked with me through it all.

I see you, too, at the beginning of Time and Space. I see you illuminating all realms of Creation with no more than your thought and energetic presence.

"You are the miracle we celebrate today!"

I hear these words echoing through for you, now. Directly, for you. They flow from all divine planes of consciousness, and complete themselves with the addition of these gentle words:

"We see you."

Their love for you is pure and immeasurable. They see the truth of your soul, as it is, without any need for you to ever be more than you most genuinely are.

> *"The imperfections you see in yourself are but illusion and mistruth. Will you free yourself from them now, so that you might see yourself as we see you? You are Light, embodied. You are bound by nothing!"*

> **~ Divine Spirit**

Will you believe in all you already are?

It takes bravery, I know. But this is what you are here for—to remember and to know.

Your *Divine Self* isn't something you'll find because another introduces you to that pristine aspect of yourself. It's something that you'll trust in when you know, beyond doubt, that you already are perfect and pure, as you are.

It's a truth that awakens when you are ready to see clearly.

> *"There's a moment when a Lotus recognizes its greater truth. It recognizes its miraculous beauty and boundless potential, and it changes nothing! It is only the knowledge—the intimate knowing of being all things—that naturally shifts the worlds of experience, within and throughout."*

> ~ **Divine Spirit**

About the Author

Alania Starhawk is a divine channel, sacred visionary, and spiritual mentor. Her gifts of clear sight and intuitive knowing allow her to connect to the infinite realms of truth and light that exist within all forms of creation. She brings valuable insights and awareness to our own greatest potential and power, while also inspiring us to move beyond all forms of limited identity and insecurity.

Alania introduces us to a world of infinite possibility by powerfully sharing the sacred teachings that speak to our soul. These enlightened teachings, which support humanity's evolution and awakening, come from the many beings of Light that communicate directly to Alania.

Alania has been professionally facilitating private mentoring sessions and inspired group experiences since 2008. Her passion is in supporting all who are ready for their own "soul expansion." She gracefully does this by connecting our hearts to universal consciousness. She reminds us that we are our own empowered and sacred source.

Alania is especially adept at clearing all limited programming, healing karmic relationships, and accessing archetypal memories in the akashic field of light. She works with sacred masters and guardians to access only that which is ready for compassionate healing and energetic activation. She brings harmony and wholeness to all infinite aspects of our sacred and divine Self.

Learn more about Alania on her website:

www.AlaniaStarhawk.com

www.ingramcontent.com/pod-product-compliance
Lightning Source LLC
Chambersburg PA
CBHW062057080426
42734CB00012B/2676